RACE WINNER!

A cockpit guide to faster sailing

Ian Nicolson
&
Richard Nicolson

ADLARD COLES
8 Grafton Street, London W1

Adlard Coles
William Collins Sons & Co. Ltd
8 Grafton Street, London W1X 3LA

First published in Great Britain by
Adlard Coles Ltd 1989
Reprinted 1990

British Library Cataloguing in Publication Data

Nicolson, Ian
   Race winner!: a cockpit guide to faster
   sailing.
   1. Racing sailing boats. Racing – Manuals
   I. Title   II. Nicolson, Richard
   797.1′4

ISBN 0–229–11834–8

Typeset by Ace Filmsetting Ltd, Frome, Somerset
Printed and bound in Great Britain by
Hartnolls Ltd, Bodmin, Cornwall

Dedication

To Denis, Alison, Hamish, Fiona, Simon and Rachel Jackson.
Especially Simon, for crewing for us, and for help in technical matters.

CONTENTS

Find out the wind speed.
Decide on the course, relative to the wind. Is it:

- **Close hauled**
- **Close reach**
- **Broad reach**
- **Quartering wind**
- **Dead run**

Turn to the correct page, and read off the settings. For instance: If the wind speed is 8 knots, and the course a close reach, turn to page 12.

Before the race the boat must be:

1. Properly prepared. See pages 53–57.
2. Got ready for the start. See page 58.
3. Taken out for plenty of practice. Follow pages 5–51 to learn about the correct settings and tensions for halyards, sheets etc.
4. The best close hauled location for the headsail sheet lead slide (or carriage or car, as some people call it) must be found by using page 52.

During practice and during a race:

If the boat is doing well write down all the settings, tensions etc on the appropriate page for future use.

If the boat is doing badly alter one item at a time, and look for an improvement. If there is a loss of speed try making the alteration the other way i.e. if tightening causes a loss of speed, try slackening. One alteration may have more than one effect. For instance, tightening in the headsail sheet will not only flatten that sail, it may also cause backwinding to the mainsail which may then need flattening.

As a rough guide, when 'small boats' are mentioned it means craft up to about 30 feet (9 metres). 'Medium-sized' racing boats are up to about 50 feet (15 metres), and 'large boats' above that approximate size.

IF YOU ARE A BEGINNER: Follow the book at first, and build up a store of experience. Note down settings, tensions, and positions on the appropriate page, when you find out which is best for your boat and rig.

IF YOU ARE AN EXPERT: Use the book as a reminder. Be honest. How many times have you been afloat and in the excitement of a race forgotten to alter one of the controls just because either:

a) everyone aboard thought someone else had 'tweaked' it, or
b) the whole crew was so busy concentrating on another boat, or the course, or a nearby squall, that one of the controls was forgotten?

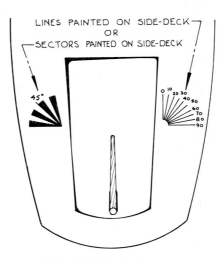

ALTERNATIVE SIGHT LINES ON THE DECK

Overstanding a mark, or sailing under the stern of a starboard tack boat unnecessarily are maddening ways of losing ground. What everyone wants is a method of assessing when to tack. Nothing works like costly complex electronic gadgets . . . or lots of practice, but a set of lines painted on deck at 10° intervals is a help.

Some people find a batch of close spaced thin lines confusing, and prefer black 'sectors' as shown on the port side-deck.

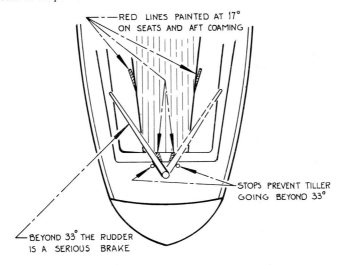

REDUCING RUDDER DRAG

Every time the helmsman uses the rudder to turn the boat, however slightly, extra resistance is caused which is likely to slow the boat. Pulling the tiller over more than about 17° is likely to give a notable increase in drag without a commensurate speeding up of the change of course.

Once the boat is actually turning the rudder can be eased over to 33°. Beyond this angle the rudder acts progressively more as a brake and less as a device for altering course. So lines on the deck, and physical stops at 33°, should help the boat go faster.

Strong winds

Just what constitutes a wind which is *too* strong for racing varies from boat to boat, from crew to crew. Many dinghies give up, quite rightly, as Force 6 gusts make things too risky. Family cruisers, especially if there are young children or beginners aboard, sensibly stop racing when it blows up to Force 7. Even quite experienced crews of 30 footers pack up when they are offshore and it is clearly blasting a good Force 8. They are doing the right thing; retiring before anything breaks or there is trouble. Relatively few people take the risk of setting a spinnaker in this wind speed.

By the time the wind is up to Force 9 only tough experienced crews in rugged well-designed boats should keep going. A small mistake in these conditions results in big trouble. Setting the spinnaker in these conditions must be a most carefully calculated risk. If in doubt, don't do it.

Racing in Force 10 is for the experts – the really knowledgeable hardened crews with no one aboard who is in any way a passenger.

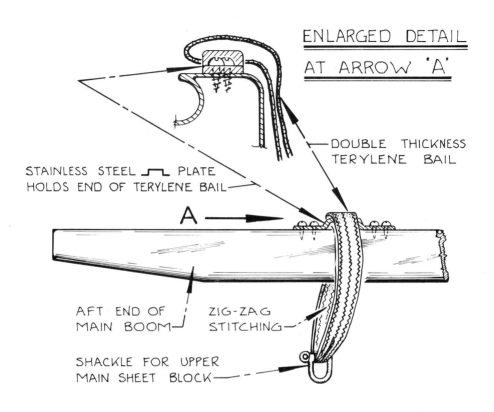

ENLARGED DETAIL
AT ARROW 'A'

DOUBLE THICKNESS
TERYLENE BAIL

STAINLESS STEEL ⌐⌐ PLATE
HOLDS END OF TERYLENE BAIL

A ➡

AFT END OF
MAIN BOOM

ZIG-ZAG
STITCHING

SHACKLE FOR UPPER
MAIN SHEET BLOCK

One way to save weight is to make things out of light materials. Normally the fittings on the spars are of stainless steel, but the usual boom bail for the main sheet can be of terylene (dacron) instead of metal.

Beaufort Scale: 0–1
Wind velocity: 0–3 knots (0–1.5 metres/second)
Pressure: 0–0.01 lb/sq foot (0–0.049 kilos/sq metre)

MAINSAIL

Shape slightly less than maximum curvature.
Top batten parallel to boom.
Halyard: Slack. Accept wrinkles on luff.
Main outhaul: Slight tension to avoid maximum fullness. Accept slight wrinkles.
Luff cunningham: Not in use.
Leech cunningham: Not in use.
Main sheet: Very loose.
Boom angle: About 5° off centreline. Approx $\frac{1}{11}$ of boom length.
Main sheet traveller: To windward.

HEADSAIL

Drifter or light No. 1 genoa. Shape slightly less than maximum curvature.
Halyard: Slack. Wrinkles just out.
Luff cunningham: Not in use.
Sheet: Haul in till sail almost touches crosstree.
Sheet lead: Locate to ensure headsail leech is parallel to mainsail.
Barber hauler: Haul inwards so that sheet tension is low. For masthead rig sheet angle is approx 9°–10°; for ¾ rig 7°–8°.
Leech line: Slack, but tight enough to prevent leech sag off, or fluttering.

PERMANENT BACKSTAY

Tension till mast bend is about ½ the fore and aft diameter, or less.

KICKING STRAP (VANG)

No tension, except in a lop, when slight tension is used to steady boom.

WEATHER RUNNER

Slight tension to ensure full mainsail on masthead rig. Very slight tension on ¾ rig.

CREW POSITION

Forward and to leeward to reduce wetted surface.

BEST SETTINGS FOUND BY TRIAL:

MAINSAIL _____	Main reef _____
Main halyard _____	Outhaul _____
Luff cunningham _____	Leech cunningham _____
Main sheet _____	Boom angle _____
Sheet traveller _____	Leech line _____
Other items _____	
HEADSAIL _____	Halyard _____
Luff cunningham _____	Leech line _____
Sheet lead _____	Barber hauler _____
Spinnaker pole height _____	Pole angle _____
Permanent backstay _____	Runner _____
Kicking strap (vang) _____	Other items _____

Beaufort Scale: 0–1
Wind velocity: 0–3 knots (0–1.5 metres/second)
Pressure: 0–0.01 lb/sq foot (0–0.049 kilos/sq metre)

MAINSAIL

Shape slightly less than maximum curvature.
Top batten parallel with boom.
Halyard: Slack. Accept wrinkles on luff.
Main outhaul: Slack or very slack. Accept slight wrinkles.
Luff cunningham: Not in use.
Leech cunningham: Not in use.
Main sheet: Very loose.
Boom angle: Ease off but keep main tell-tales flying.
Main traveller: Roughly on centreline. Use traveller not vertical pull of sheet to get right boom angle.

HEADSAIL

No. 1 Light genoa, or drifter or light reacher.
Halyard: Slack. Wrinkles just out.
Luff cunningham: Not in use.
Sheet: Eased off and outboard and forward of close hauled position. Tension low.
Sheet lead: Locate outboard of close hauled position, and so as to get all tell-tales working together.
Barber hauler: Ease clew outwards till all tell-tales work together.
Leech line: Slack but tight enough to prevent leech sag off, or fluttering.

PERMANENT BACKSTAY

Tension till mast bend is about ½ the fore and aft diameter, or less.

KICKING STRAP (VANG)

No tension, except in a lop, when slight tension is used to steady boom.

WEATHER RUNNER

Slight tension to ensure full mainsail on masthead rig. Very slight tension on ¾ rig.

CREW POSITION

Forward and to leeward to reduce wetted surface.

BEST SETTINGS FOUND BY TRIAL:

MAINSAIL _____	Main reef _____
Main halyard _____	Outhaul _____
Luff cunningham _____	Leech cunningham _____
Main sheet _____	Boom angle _____
Sheet traveller _____	Leech line _____
Other items _____	
HEADSAIL _____	Halyard _____
Luff cunningham _____	Leech line _____
Sheet lead _____	Barber hauler _____
Spinnaker pole height _____	Pole angle _____
Permanent backstay _____	Runner _____
Kicking strap (vang) _____	Other items _____

Beaufort Scale: 0–1
Wind velocity: 0–3 knots (0–1.5 metres/second)
Pressure: 0–0.01 lb/sq foot (0–0.049 kilos/sq metre)

MAINSAIL

Shape at or near maximum curvature.
Top batten parallel with boom.
Halyard: Slack. Accept wrinkles in luff.
Main outhaul: Slack especially when wind is aft off 60° of centreline.
Leechline: Try slight tension to increase camber.
Luff cunningham: Not in use.
Leech cunningham: Not in use.
Main sheet: Very loose. Start with boom angle at 45° and adjust till tell-tales all
   stream aft.
Main traveller: At or near outboard end of slide. Use traveller, where possible,
   rather than main sheet to get right boom angle.
Boom guy: Fitted to hold boom off and steady.

HEADSAIL

Medium spinnaker or light reacher. Maybe add staysail.
Halyard: For spinnaker, keep sail slightly off mast to prevent 'choking'. For
   reacher, just take wrinkles out of luff.
Sheet: For spinnaker guy locate pole roughly 15° off forestay. Trim sheet so
   that both clews are level. For reacher slack sheet well off, outward location
   of sheet lead.
Barber hauler: Right off.
Reacher leech line: May be tightened to increase camber.

PERMANENT BACKSTAY

Tension just on for full mainsail.

KICKING STRAP (VANG)

No tension except in lop, when slight tension is used to steady boom.

WEATHER RUNNER

Moderate to slight tension to ensure full mainsail on masthead rig. Very slight
   tension on ¾ rig.

CREW POSITION

Forward and to leeward to reduce wetted surface.

BEST SETTINGS FOUND BY TRIAL:

MAINSAIL _____	Main reef _____
Main halyard _____	Outhaul _____
Luff cunningham _____	Leech cunningham _____
Main sheet _____	Boom angle _____
Sheet traveller _____	Leech line _____
Other items _____	
HEADSAIL _____	Halyard _____
Luff cunningham _____	Leech line _____
Sheet lead _____	Barber hauler _____
Spinnaker pole height _____	Pole angle _____
Permanent backstay _____	Runner _____
Kicking strap (vang) _____	Other items _____

Beaufort Scale: 0–1
Wind velocity: 0–3 knots (0–1.5 metres/second)
Pressure: 0–0.01 lb/sq foot (0–0.049 kilos/sq metre)

MAINSAIL

Shape at or near maximum curvature.
Top batten not far off boom angle.
Halyard: Tension to give maximum sail area (i.e. firmly tight) but retain full shape.
Main outhaul: Slack right off, but not so as to lose effective sail area.
Leech line: Try slight tension to increase camber.
Luff cunningham: Not in use.
Leech cunningham: Not in use.
Main sheet: Very loose. Start with boom off 75° to centreline and adjust till tell-tales all stream.
Main sheet traveller: Right outboard.
Boom foreguy: Fit one to keep boom forward and steady.

HEADSAIL

Light or very light spinnaker.
Halyard: Tight up except in very light airs, when the top of the sail should be slightly away from the masthead.
Sheet and guy trimmed to give level clews, and spinnaker boom at right angles to wind. Spinnaker boom low for maximum effective sail area.

PERMANENT BACKSTAY

Tension just on.

KICKING STRAP (VANG)

Moderate tension to give maximum effective sail area, limit twist, and keep boom steady in a lop.

WEATHER RUNNER

Moderate to slight tension to ensure full mainsail on masthead rig. Very slight tension on ¾ rig.

CREW POSITION

Forward and to windward to reduce wetted surface.

BEST SETTINGS FOUND BY TRIAL:

MAINSAIL _____	Main reef _____
Main halyard _____	Outhaul _____
Luff cunningham _____	Leech cunningham _____
Main sheet _____	Boom angle _____
Sheet traveller _____	Leech line _____
Other items _____	
HEADSAIL _____	Halyard _____
Luff cunningham _____	Leech line _____
Sheet lead _____	Barber hauler _____
Spinnaker pole height _____	Pole angle _____
Permanent backstay _____	Runner _____
Kicking strap (vang) _____	Other items _____

Beaufort Scale: 0–1
Wind velocity: 0–3 knots (0–1.5 metres/second)
Pressure: 0–0.01 lb/sq foot (0–0.049 kilos/sq metre)

MAINSAIL

Shape at or near maximum curvature.
Top batten not far off boom angle.
Halyard: Tension to give maximum sail area, i.e. firmly tight, but retain full
    shape.
Main outhaul: Slack right off, but not so much as to lose effective sail area.
Leech line: Try slight tension to increase camber.
Luff cunningham: Not in use.
Leech cunningham: Not in use.
Main sheet: Slack right off till boom almost touches shrouds.
Boom foreguy: Fit one to hold boom forward and steady.
Mainsheet traveller: Right outboard.

HEADSAIL

Light or very light spinnaker or floater.
Halyard: Tight up except in very light airs when the top of the sail should be
    slightly away from the masthead.
Sheet and guy trimmed to give level clews, and spinnaker boom at right angles
    to hull centreline.
Spinnaker boom low for maximum effective area.

PERMANENT BACKSTAY

Ease tension right off to get mast upright.

KICKING STRAP (VANG)

Moderate tension to give maximum effective sail area, limit twist, and steady
    boom in a lop.

WEATHER RUNNER

Tension to give straight mast, or on masthead rig even a slight bend aft in the
    middle and hence fuller mainsail.

CREW POSITION

Forward and to windward to reduce wetted surface.

IT OFTEN PAYS TO TACK DOWNWIND, RATHER THAN RUN DEAD DOWNWIND.

BEST SETTINGS FOUND BY TRIAL:

MAINSAIL _____	Main reef _____
Main halyard _____	Outhaul _____
Luff cunningham _____	Leech cunningham _____
Main sheet _____	Boom angle _____
Sheet traveller _____	Leech line _____
Other items _____	
HEADSAIL _____	Halyard _____
Luff cunningham _____	Leech line _____
Sheet lead _____	Barber hauler _____
Spinnaker pole height _____	Pole angle _____
Permanent backstay _____	Runner _____
Kicking strap (vang) _____	Other items _____

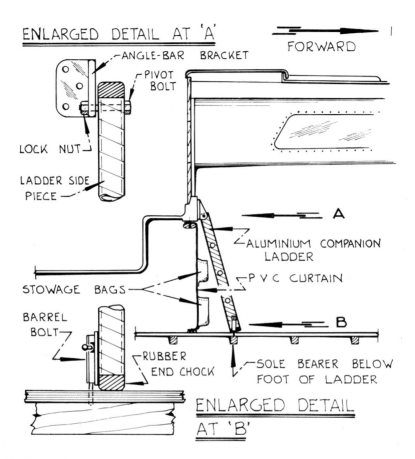

ENLARGED DETAIL AT 'A'

FORWARD

ANGLE-BAR BRACKET

PIVOT BOLT

LOCK NUT

LADDER SIDE PIECE

A

ALUMINIUM COMPANION LADDER

P V C CURTAIN

STOWAGE BAGS

BARREL BOLT

B

RUBBER END CHOCK

SOLE BEARER BELOW FOOT OF LADDER

ENLARGED DETAIL AT 'B'

CABIN STEPS

When building or changing a racing boat, weight saving is all important. The steps into the cabin can be cheaply made from a length of standard aluminium ladder or, for anyone who likes wider treads, from a set of household steps.

Handy stowage is important and a light way to achieve it is to have cloth stowage bags which may be sewn to the cloth casing round the engine. PVC cloth is waterproof but some owners prefer terylene (dacron) and choose the tanned colour as it does not show the dirt.

Beaufort Scale: 2–3
Wind velocity: 4–10 knots (2.1–5.1 metres/second)
Pressure: 0.08–0.28 lb/sq foot (0.39–1.37 kilos/sq metre)

MAINSAIL
All tell-tales flying except top one which flies for ¾ of the time.
Flattening reef. Top batten parallel with boom.
Halyard: Tight enough to just eliminate luff wrinkles.
Main outhaul: Moderate tension.
Leech line: As slack as possible but avoid leech sag off, or flutter.
Luff cunningham: Slight tension at top of this wind force.
Leech cunningham: Not in use.
Main sheet: Boom at between 0°–5° to leeward to give between 3°–5° weather
   helm. Sheet not tight down.
Main sheet traveller: Near centreline.

HEADSAIL
Light No. 1 genoa.
Halyard: Tension firm. Luff creases eliminated.
Luff cunningham: Tension down between 10% and 20% at top end of this wind
   speed.
Sheet: Trim in till headsail is near crosstree end.
Barber hauler: Sheet lead angle off centreline for masthead rig 7°–10°. Sheet
   lead angle off centreline for ¾ rig 7°–8°.
Leech line: Slack off but avoid sag to leeward or leech flutter.

PERMANENT BACKSTAY
Tension roughly between ¹⁄₁₀ and ⅙ breaking strain, or to give mast bend about
   equal to mast fore and aft diameter.

KICKING STRAP (VANG)
Not needed, except slightly sometimes, to flatten mainsail.

WEATHER RUNNER
About half tension but avoid over-tightening on masthead rig; aim to limit mast
   bend. Moderate tension on ¾ rig for straight forestay.

CREW POSITION
On windward side and forward.

BEST SETTINGS FOUND BY TRIAL:

MAINSAIL _____	Main reef _____
Main halyard _____	Outhaul _____
Luff cunningham _____	Leech cunningham _____
Main sheet _____	Boom angle _____
Sheet traveller _____	Leech line _____
Other items _____	
HEADSAIL _____	Halyard _____
Luff cunningham _____	Leech line _____
Sheet lead _____	Barber hauler _____
Spinnaker pole height _____	Pole angle _____
Permanent backstay _____	Runner _____
Kicking strap (vang) _____	Other items _____

Beaufort Scale: 2–3
Wind velocity: 4–10 knots (2.1–5.1 metres/second)
Pressure: 0.08–0.28 lb/sq foot (0.39–1.37 kilos/sq metre)

MAINSAIL

Flattening reef tightened in. Top batten parallel with boom.
Halyard: Tight enough to eliminate most luff wrinkles, or slightly less than close hauled tension.
Main outhaul: Moderate tension.
Luff cunningham: Slight tension at top of this wind force.
Leech cunningham: Not in use.
Main sheet: Boom off about 15° and trimmed to get all tell-tales flying. Sheet moderately tight.
Main sheet traveller: Near centreline.

HEADSAIL

Light No. 1 genoa or reacher.
Halyard: Tension firm. Luff creases just eliminated.
Luff cunningham: Tension down between 10% and 20% at top end of this wind speed.
Sheet: Ease off, forward and outboard of close hauled position, with leech parallel to mainsail.
Barber hauler: Ease outboard to avoid backwinding mainsail.
Leech line: Slack off but avoid sag to leeward or leech flutter.

PERMANENT BACKSTAY

Tension roughly between $\frac{1}{16}$ and $\frac{1}{8}$ breaking strain, or to give mast bend about equal to $\frac{3}{4}$ of mast fore and aft diameter.

KICKING STRAP (VANG)

Slight tension.

WEATHER RUNNER

About half tension but avoid overtightening on masthead rig; aim to limit mast bend. Moderate tension for $\frac{3}{4}$ rig for straight forestay.

CREW POSITION

On windward side amidships.

BEST SETTINGS FOUND BY TRIAL:

MAINSAIL _____	Main reef _____
Main halyard _____	Outhaul _____
Luff cunningham _____	Leech cunningham _____
Main sheet _____	Boom angle _____
Sheet traveller _____	Leech line _____
Other items _____	
HEADSAIL _____	Halyard _____
Luff cunningham _____	Leech line _____
Sheet lead _____	Barber hauler _____
Spinnaker pole height _____	Pole angle _____
Permanent backstay _____	Runner _____
Kicking strap (vang) _____	Other items _____

Beaufort Scale: 2–3
Wind velocity: 4–10 knots (2.1–5.1 metres/second)
Pressure: 0.08–0.28 lb/sq foot (0.39–1.37 kilos/sq metre)

MAINSAIL
Halyard: Tight enough to eliminate most luff wrinkles.
Main outhaul: Ease off when apparent wind is 55° off or more, to open foot shelf.
Leech line: May be slightly tensioned to increase sail camber.
Luff cunningham: Not in use.
Leech cunningham: Not in use.
Main sheet: Boom off about 45° to get all tell-tales streaming.
Main sheet traveller: Well off, probably fully off.
Boom guy: Fit one in a lop to hold boom off and steady.

HEADSAIL
Starcut spinnaker, or medium spinnaker, or reacher. Maybe add staysail.
Halyard: Tight up, except for reacher which needs only moderate luff tension.
Sheet: Trim spinnaker sheet constantly to keep luff just not curling inwards. Boom guy as far back as possible without sail collapse. Boom end slightly below leeward clew. Sheet the reacher as far outboard as possible. As the wind increases the sheet lead goes forward. Try to keep all tell-tales flying together. If upper tell-tales break first move lead forward.
Barber hauler: Right outboard.
Leech line: Slight or moderate tension, or just occasionally high tension to increase camber of reacher.

PERMANENT BACKSTAY
Slight tension to reduce mast bend to a minimum.

KICKING STRAP (VANG)
Tension on to take over from main sheet traveller.

WEATHER RUNNER
Moderate tension to keep mast straight.

CREW POSITION
On windward side and aft of amidships.

BEST SETTINGS FOUND BY TRIAL:

MAINSAIL _____	Main reef _____
Main halyard _____	Outhaul _____
Luff cunningham _____	Leech cunningham _____
Main sheet _____	Boom angle _____
Sheet traveller _____	Leech line _____
Other items _____	
HEADSAIL _____	Halyard _____
Luff cunningham _____	Leech line _____
Sheet lead _____	Barber hauler _____
Spinnaker pole height _____	Pole angle _____
Permanent backstay _____	Runner _____
Kicking strap (vang) _____	Other items _____

Beaufort Scale: 2–3
Wind velocity: 4–10 knots (2.1–5.1 metres/second)
Pressure: 0.08–0.28 lb/sq foot (0.39–1.37 kilos/sq metre)

MAINSAIL
Halyard: Tight enough to eliminate luff wrinkles.
Main outhaul: Eased well off.
Leech line: May be well tensioned to increase sail camber.
Main sheet: Slack off till boom is about 75° off then trim to get all tell-tales
    flying.
Main sheet traveller: Right off to leeward.
Boom foreguy: Fit one to hold boom forward and steady.

HEADSAIL
Light or medium spinnaker.
Halyard: Tight up.
Sheet: Spinnaker constantly trimmed to keep luff just not curling inwards.
    Clews level.
Spinnaker boom: Moderately high, and at 90° to the apparent wind.

PERMANENT BACKSTAY
Slight tension to reduce mast bend to minimum.

KICKING STRAP (VANG)
Tension on to take over from main sheet traveller.

WINDWARD RUNNER
Slight tension on masthead and ¾ rig to suit mast bend.

CREW POSITION
Located to keep boat upright and level. Spread weight athwartships to
    minimise rolling.

BEST SETTINGS FOUND BY TRIAL:

MAINSAIL _____	Main reef _____
Main halyard _____	Outhaul _____
Luff cunningham _____	Leech cunningham _____
Main sheet _____	Boom angle _____
Sheet traveller _____	Leech line _____
Other items _____	
HEADSAIL _____	Halyard _____
Luff cunningham _____	Leech line _____
Sheet lead _____	Barber hauler _____
Spinnaker pole height _____	Pole angle _____
Permanent backstay _____	Runner _____
Kicking strap (vang) _____	Other items _____

Beaufort Scale: 2–3
Wind velocity: 4–10 knots (2.1–5.1 metres/second)
Pressure: 0.08–0.28 lb/sq foot (0.39–1.37 kilos/sq metre)

MAINSAIL
Halyard: Tight up.
Main outhaul: Eased well off.
Leech line: May be well tensioned to increase sail camber.
Main sheet: Slacked off till boom is near shrouds.
Main sheet traveller: Right off to leeward.
Boom foreguy: Fit one to hold boom forward and steady.

HEADSAIL
Light or medium spinnaker.
Halyard: Tight up.
Spinnaker sheet: Slack off till clews are level. Trim constantly to keep luff just
    not curling inwards.
Spinnaker boom: Moderately high, at right angles to apparent wind.

PERMANENT BACKSTAY
Slight tension to reduce mast bend to a minimum.

KICKING STRAP (VANG)
Tension slightly eased from maximum.

WINDWARD RUNNER
Slight tension on masthead and ¾ rig to suit mast bend.

CREW POSITION
Located to keep boat upright and level. Spread weight athwartships to
    minimise rolling.

IT OFTEN PAYS TO TACK DOWNWIND, RATHER THAN RUN DEAD DOWNWIND.

BEST SETTINGS FOUND BY TRIAL:

MAINSAIL _____	Main reef _____
Main halyard _____	Outhaul _____
Luff cunningham _____	Leech cunningham _____
Main sheet _____	Boom angle _____
Sheet traveller _____	Leech line _____
Other items _____	
HEADSAIL _____	Halyard _____
Luff cunningham _____	Leech line _____
Sheet lead _____	Barber hauler _____
Spinnaker pole height _____	Pole angle _____
Permanent backstay _____	Runner _____
Kicking strap (vang) _____	Other items _____

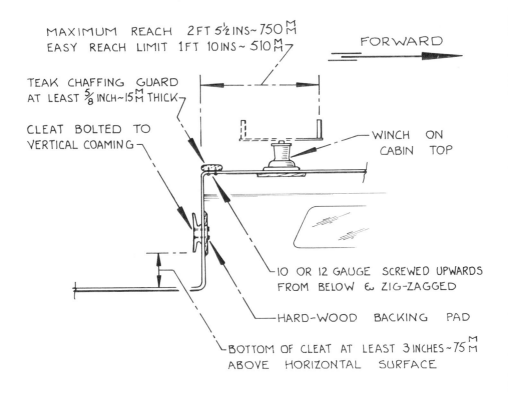

MAXIMUM REACH 2FT 5½INS~750 M
EASY REACH LIMIT 1FT 10INS~510 M

FORWARD

TEAK CHAFFING GUARD
AT LEAST ⅝INCH~15 M THICK

CLEAT BOLTED TO
VERTICAL COAMING

WINCH ON
CABIN TOP

10 OR 12 GAUGE SCREWED UPWARDS
FROM BELOW & ZIG-ZAGGED

HARD-WOOD BACKING PAD

BOTTOM OF CLEAT AT LEAST 3 INCHES~75 M
ABOVE HORIZONTAL SURFACE

PROTECTING FIBREGLASS

Where a rope rubs over fibreglass it will soon chafe through and can cause serious damage in the course of a weekend. Though protection strips made of metal last indefinitely, they are not so easy to make and fit as wood guards. The wood may chafe through in time but it is easy to replace.

Where ropes lead aft along the cabin top, it is often worth fitting a traditional cleat or two on the vertical coaming because some 'instant' cleats are not completely reliable.

Beaufort Scale: 4–5
Wind velocity: 11–20 knots (5.5–10.3 metres/second)
Pressure: 0.67–1.31 lb/sq foot (3.27–6.39 kilos/sq metre)

MAINSAIL
Flattening reef. Small yachts may have first reef in.
Top batten between parallel with boom and 10° off.
At lower wind speed top tell-tale flies ¾ of the time.
Halyard: Tight up, to about ⅓ breaking strain.
Main outhaul: Fully or nearly fully tensioned.
Luff cunningham: Typically quarter down or thereabouts.
Leech cunningham: Quarter or half tight, and tighter still at top of this wind
    range.
Main sheet: Tight in. Boom between 0°–5° to leeward of centreline, to give
    between 3°–5° of weather helm.
Main sheet traveller: Near centreline, but ease off to reduce weather helm.

HEADSAIL
Heavy No. 1 or No. 2 (particularly on small yachts).
Halyard: Tight up, to approx ⅓ breaking strain.
Luff cunningham: Typically between 30% and 70% tight down.
Sheet: Trim in till headsail is close to crosstree end.
Barber hauler: Sheet lead angle off centreline for masthead rig 8°–10°. For ¾
    rig 8°–9°.
Leech line: Slack off but avoid sag to leeward or leech flutter.

PERMANENT BACKSTAY
Tension roughly between ⅙ and ⅓ breaking strain, or to induce mast bend
    equal to about twice the mast's fore and aft diameter.

KICKING STRAP (VANG)
Not needed, except slightly sometimes, to flatten mainsail.

WINDWARD RUNNER
For masthead rig apply moderate tension to limit mast bend. For ¾ rig apply
    high tension for straight forestay.

CREW POSITION
Forward and to windward.

BEST SETTINGS FOUND BY TRIAL:

MAINSAIL _____	Main reef _____
Main halyard _____	Outhaul _____
Luff cunningham _____	Leech cunningham _____
Main sheet _____	Boom angle _____
Sheet traveller _____	Leech line _____
Other items _____	
HEADSAIL _____	Halyard _____
Luff cunningham _____	Leech line _____
Sheet lead _____	Barber hauler _____
Spinnaker pole height _____	Pole angle _____
Permanent backstay _____	Runner _____
Kicking strap (vang) _____	Other items _____

Beaufort Scale: 4–5
Wind velocity: 11–20 knots (5.5–10.3 metres/second)
Pressure: 0.67–1.31 lb/sq foot (3.27–6.39 kilos/sq metre)

MAINSAIL

Flattening reef. Small yachts may have first reef in.
Top batten between parallel with boom and 10° off.
Halyard: Tight up, to about ¼ breaking strain, or slightly less than close hauled
tension.
Main outhaul: Fully or nearly fully tensioned. (Fully tensioned at top end of
wind band.)
Luff cunningham: Quarter down or thereabouts.
Leech cunningham: Fully or nearly fully tight.
Main sheet: Tight in. Boom off to get all tell-tales streaming.
Main sheet traveller: Off to leeward so as to be nearly under boom. Ease to
reduce weather helm.

HEADSAIL

Heavy No. 1 genoa, or No. 2 (particularly on small yachts).
Halyard: Tight up, to approx ¼ breaking strain, or enough to give slight extra
fullness, compared with close hauled shape.
Luff cunningham: Typically between 30% and 70% tight down.
Sheet: Ease off, forward and outboard of close hauled position, with leech par-
allel to mainsail.
Barber hauler: Ease outboard to avoid backwinding mainsail.
Leech line: Slack off but avoid sag to leeward or leech flutter.

PERMANENT BACKSTAY

Tension roughly between ⅛ and ⅙ breaking strain, or to induce mast bend
equal to about twice the mast's fore and aft diameter. Tighten as wind rises.

KICKING STRAP (VANG)

Ease off so that main sheet and traveller control mainsail twist.

WINDWARD RUNNER

For masthead rig apply moderate tension to limit mast bend. For ¾ rig apply
high tension for straight forestay.

CREW POSITION

Forward and to windward.

BEST SETTINGS FOUND BY TRIAL:

MAINSAIL _____	Main reef _____
Main halyard _____	Outhaul _____
Luff cunningham _____	Leech cunningham _____
Main sheet _____	Boom angle _____
Sheet traveller _____	Leech line _____
Other items _____	
HEADSAIL _____	Halyard _____
Luff cunningham _____	Leech line _____
Sheet lead _____	Barber hauler _____
Spinnaker pole height _____	Pole angle _____
Permanent backstay _____	Runner _____
Kicking strap (vang) _____	Other items _____

Beaufort Scale: 4–5
Wind velocity: 11–20 knots (5.5–10.3 metres/second)
Pressure: 0.67–1.31 lb/sq foot (3.27–6.39 kilos/sq metre)

MAINSAIL

Small yachts may have first reef in.

Halyard: Tight up to about ¼ breaking strain, or less than close hauled.

Main outhaul: About half tension at low end of wind band. Fully tight at top end of band, especially as wind comes aft.

Luff cunningham: Quarter down or less.

Leech cunningham: Half tight.

Main sheet: Ease off to get tell-tales streaming. Ease further to reduce weather helm.

Main sheet traveller: Right to leeward.

HEADSAIL

Starcut spinnaker, or medium spinnaker, or reacher. Maybe add staysail.

Halyard: Tight up, except for reacher which needs only moderate tension.

Sheet: Trim spinnaker constantly to keep luff just not curling inwards. Boom guy as far back as possible without sail collapse. Boom end slightly below leeward clew. For reacher sheet well aft, but move sheet forward as wind comes aft, and aim always to have all tell-tales flying together. Sheet right outboard.

Barber hauler: Right outboard for reacher.

Leech line on reacher: Slack off but avoid leech flutter.

PERMANENT BACKSTAY

Slight tension to reduce mast bend to a minimum for masthead rig. Increase tension as wind increases. Moderate tension for ¾ rig.

KICKING STRAP (VANG)

Tight down, but ease to reduce weather helm.

WINDWARD RUNNER

About half tension to keep mast straight for spinnaker, but tight up for reacher. Slight tension for ¾ rig but increase as wind increases.

CREW POSITION

Aft and to windward.

BEST SETTINGS FOUND BY TRIAL:

MAINSAIL _____	Main reef _____
Main halyard _____	Outhaul _____
Luff cunningham _____	Leech cunningham _____
Main sheet _____	Boom angle _____
Sheet traveller _____	Leech line _____
Other items _____	
HEADSAIL _____	Halyard _____
Luff cunningham _____	Leech line _____
Sheet lead _____	Barber hauler _____
Spinnaker pole height _____	Pole angle _____
Permanent backstay _____	Runner _____
Kicking strap (vang) _____	Other items _____

Beaufort Scale: 4–5
Wind velocity: 11–20 knots (5.5–10.3 metres/second)
Pressure: 0.67–1.31 lb/sq foot (3.27–6.39 kilos/sq metre)

MAINSAIL
Small yachts may have first reef in.
Halyard: Tight up, but not fully to give slight extra sail camber.
Main outhaul: Eased off to about ¼ tension. Tighten as wind goes up to 20
   knots.
Luff cunningham: Not in use.
Leech cunningham: Not in use.
Main sheet: Ease off till boom is about 75° off centreline, then trim till all tell-
   tales are streaming.
Main sheet traveller: Right off to leeward.

HEADSAIL
Medium spinnaker.
Halyard: Tight up.
Sheet: Trim spinnaker constantly to keep luff just not curling inwards. Spin-
   naker boom as a general rule 90° to the apparent wind or as far back as
   possible without sail collapse. Clews level.

PERMANENT BACKSTAY
Slight tension to reduce mast bend to a minimum.

KICKING STRAP (VANG)
Tight down. Slack off as boom touches the water or weather helm increases.

WINDWARD RUNNER
Slight tension to keep mast straight on masthead rig. Moderate tension on ¾
   rig.

CREW POSITION
Aft and mainly to windward. Spread load to minimise rolling.

BEST SETTINGS FOUND BY TRIAL:

MAINSAIL _____	Main reef _____
Main halyard _____	Outhaul _____
Luff cunningham _____	Leech cunningham _____
Main sheet _____	Boom angle _____
Sheet traveller _____	Leech line _____
Other items _____	
HEADSAIL _____	Halyard _____
Luff cunningham _____	Leech line _____
Sheet lead _____	Barber hauler _____
Spinnaker pole height _____	Pole angle _____
Permanent backstay _____	Runner _____
Kicking strap (vang) _____	Other items _____

Beaufort Scale: 4–5
Wind velocity: 11–20 knots (5.5–10.3 metres/second)
Pressure: 0.67–1.31 lb/sq foot (3.27–6.39 kilos/sq metre)

MAINSAIL
Small yachts may have first reef in.
Halyard: Almost fully tight, but eased enough to give slightly more sail camber.
Main outhaul: Eased off to ¼ tension or less.
Luff cunningham: Not in use.
Leech cunningham: Not in use.
Main sheet: Ease off till boom is near shrouds.
Main sheet traveller: Right off to leeward.

HEADSAIL
Medium spinnaker.
Halyard: Tight up.
Sheet: Slack off till clews are level. Sheet and guy led well forward, e.g. just aft
    of amidships. As wind increases ease guy forward to stop rolling.
Spinnaker boom high, and at right angles to apparent wind.

PERMANENT BACKSTAY
Slight tension to keep mast straight.

KICKING STRAP (VANG)
Tight up. Ease if boom touches water or boat starts to broach.

WINDWARD RUNNER
Slight tension on masthead rig to keep mast straight. Moderate tension on ¾
    rig.

CREW POSITION
Aft. Weight spread out to minimise rolling.

IT OFTEN PAYS TO TACK DOWNWIND, RATHER THAN RUN DEAD DOWNWIND.

BEST SETTINGS FOUND BY TRIAL:

MAINSAIL _____	Main reef _____
Main halyard _____	Outhaul _____
Luff cunningham _____	Leech cunningham _____
Main sheet _____	Boom angle _____
Sheet traveller _____	Leech line _____
Other items _____	
HEADSAIL _____	Halyard _____
Luff cunningham _____	Leech line _____
Sheet lead _____	Barber hauler _____
Spinnaker pole height _____	Pole angle _____
Permanent backstay _____	Runner _____
Kicking strap (vang) _____	Other items _____

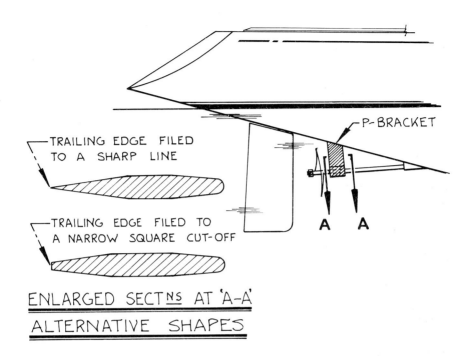

TRAILING EDGE FILED TO A SHARP LINE

TRAILING EDGE FILED TO A NARROW SQUARE CUT-OFF

P-BRACKET

A A

ENLARGED SECT^NS AT 'A-A'

ALTERNATIVE SHAPES

P-BRACKET FAIRING

The resistance of any 'plate' in water can be reduced if the trailing edge is fined away to a knife sharpness. This takes lots of work and it may weaken a fitting like a P-bracket. The second best way to minimise the drag is to finish the trailing edge off with a sharp, square-cut edge, which should be as narrow as possible. This is shown in the bottom enlarged section.

Beaufort Scale: 6
Wind velocity: 21–26 knots (10.6–13 metres/second)
Pressure: 2.30 lb/sq foot (11.22 kilos/sq metre)

MAINSAIL
Small yachts have 2 reefs, others 1 reef.
Top batten about 15° further off than boom. For large yachts with no reefs, luff
  and leech cunninghams both fully tight.
Halyard: Tight up to about ⅓ breaking strain.
Main sheet: Tight down, with boom off about 8°.
Main sheet traveller: Slide to leeward enough to give boom 8° off centreline
  with tight main sheet. Ease off to reduce weather helm.

HEADSAIL
No. 2 genoa, or in small yachts No. 3 genoa.
Halyard: Tight up to approx ⅓ breaking strain.
Sheet: Sheet tight in till sail is near but not on crosstrees.
Barber hauler: Sheet lead angle off centreline between 9° and 12°, further out
  for stronger winds.
Leech line: Just tight enough to avoid flutter.

PERMANENT BACKSTAY
Tension high, typically about ⅓ breaking strain, on masthead rig for straight
  forestay and on ¾ rig for straight forestay and flat mainsail.

KICKING STRAP (VANG)
Not needed, except sometimes, to flatten mainsail.

WINDWARD RUNNER
Moderately tight on masthead rig. Fully tight for straight forestay on ¾ rig.

CREW POSITION
To windward and forward.

BEST SETTINGS FOUND BY TRIAL:

MAINSAIL _____   Main reef _____
Main halyard _____   Outhaul _____
Luff cunningham _____   Leech cunningham _____
Main sheet _____   Boom angle _____
Sheet traveller _____   Leech line _____
Other items _____
HEADSAIL _____   Halyard _____
Luff cunningham _____   Leech line _____
Sheet lead _____   Barber hauler _____
Spinnaker pole height _____   Pole angle _____
Permanent backstay _____   Runner _____
Kicking strap (vang) _____   Other items _____

Beaufort Scale: 6
Wind velocity: 21–26 knots (10.6–13 metres/second)
Pressure: 2.30 lb/sq foot (11.22 kilos/sq metre)

MAINSAIL

Small yachts have 2 reefs, others 1 reef.

Top batten slightly further off the wind than boom. For large yachts which might have no reefs, luff and leech cunninghams both fully tight.

Halyard: Tight up to about ⅓ breaking strain.

Main sheet: Tight down, but eased slightly in squalls to reduce weather helm, and feather off top of sail.

Main sheet traveller: Boom off typically 20° but adjusted to suit course. Ease to leeward to reduce weather helm, especially in squalls.

HEADSAIL

No. 2 genoa, or in small yachts No. 3 genoa.

Halyard: Tight up to approx ⅓ breaking strain.

Sheet: Ease off, forward and outboard of close hauled position, with leech made parallel to mainsail.

Barber hauler: Ease outboard to avoid backwinding mainsail.

Leech line: Just tight enough to avoid flutter.

PERMANENT BACKSTAY

Tension roughly between ⅕ and ⅓ breaking strain, or to induce mast bend equal to about twice the mast's fore and aft diameter.

KICKING STRAP (VANG)

Ease off slightly so that main sheet and traveller control mainsail twist.

WINDWARD RUNNER

Well up but not fully, to accord with mast bend on a masthead rig. Fully tight for straight forestay on ¾ rig.

CREW POSITION

To windward and forward.

BEST SETTINGS FOUND BY TRIAL:

MAINSAIL _____	Main reef _____
Main halyard _____	Outhaul _____
Luff cunningham _____	Leech cunningham _____
Main sheet _____	Boom angle _____
Sheet traveller _____	Leech line _____
Other items _____	
HEADSAIL _____	Halyard _____
Luff cunningham _____	Leech line _____
Sheet lead _____	Barber hauler _____
Spinnaker pole height _____	Pole angle _____
Permanent backstay _____	Runner _____
Kicking strap (vang) _____	Other items _____

Beaufort Scale: 6
Wind velocity: 21–26 knots (10.6–13 metres/second)
Pressure: 2.30 lb/sq foot (11.22 kilos/sq metre)

MAINSAIL

Small yachts have 1 or 2 reefs, others 1 reef. Some large yachts need no reef. On
    these, have outhaul fully tight.
Top batten slightly further off the wind than the main boom.
Luff cunningham tightened down on a large yacht which has not reefed.
Halyard: Tight up to about ¼ breaking strain, or less than close hauled.
Main sheet: Eased off to get all tell-tales to stream off, with boom out roughly
    45° but to suit course. Ease off to reduce weather helm.
Main sheet traveller: Right off. Take in leeward tackle to absorb shock if yacht
    has to be gybed.

HEADSAIL

No. 2 genoa or heavy reacher (or on a small yacht No. 3 genoa) or starcut spin-
    naker or medium spinnaker.
Halyard: Tight up to approx ¼ breaking strain, for genoas. Reacher needs
    moderate halyard tension.
Sheet: On genoa or reacher ease off till headsail leech is parallel to mainsail, all
    tell-tales flying. Sheet lead will be forward and outboard of close reaching
    position. Trim spinnaker constantly to keep luff just not curling inwards.
    Boom at 90° to the wind, or just off forestay.
Barber hauler: Right to leeward.
Leech line: Just tight enough to avoid flutter.

PERMANENT BACKSTAY

Tension between ⅕ and ⅓ breaking strain, or to induce mast bend equal to
    about twice the mast fore and aft diameter.

KICKING STRAP (VANG)

Near tight up, but slackened off to ease off leech of sail, to reduce weather helm
    and heeling.

WINDWARD RUNNER

Moderately tight but eased just enough to cater for mast bend on masthead rig.
    Tight up on ¾ rig.

CREW POSITION

To windward and aft.

BEST SETTINGS FOUND BY TRIAL:

MAINSAIL _____	Main reef _____
Main halyard _____	Outhaul _____
Luff cunningham _____	Leech cunningham _____
Main sheet _____	Boom angle _____
Sheet traveller _____	Leech line _____
Other items _____	
HEADSAIL _____	Halyard _____
Luff cunningham _____	Leech line _____
Sheet lead _____	Barber hauler _____
Spinnaker pole height _____	Pole angle _____
Permanent backstay _____	Runner _____
Kicking strap (vang) _____	Other items _____

Beaufort Scale: 6
Wind velocity: 21–26 knots (10.6–13 metres/second)
Pressure: 2.30 lb/sq foot (11.22 kilos/sq metre)

MAINSAIL

Small yachts have 1 or 2 reefs: others 1 reef. However, large yachts will probably have no reefs, and others may have fewer reefs than stated, especially in sheltered waters and where other favourable factors apply.

Halyard: Tight up, but not fully, to give ample sail camber.

Main outhaul: Tight out for maximum sail area.

Main sheet: Ease off till boom is about 75° off centreline, then trim till all tell-tales are streaming.

Main sheet traveller: Right off to leeward. Take in leeward tackle to absorb shock if yacht has to be gybed.

Boom foreguy: Should be fitted.

HEADSAIL

Medium spinnaker.

Halyard: Tight up.

Sheet: Trim spinnaker constantly to keep luff just not curling inwards. Spinnaker boom as a general rule 90° to the apparent wind or as far back as possible without sail collapse. Clews level.

PERMANENT BACKSTAY

Slight tension to reduce mast bend to a minimum.

KICKING STRAP (VANG)

Tight down. Slack off as boom touches the water or weather helm increases.

WINDWARD RUNNER

Just enough to cater for mast bend on masthead rig. Moderately tight on ¾ rig.

CREW POSITION

Aft and mainly to windward. Spread load to minimise rolling.

BEST SETTINGS FOUND BY TRIAL:

MAINSAIL _____	Main reef _____
Main halyard _____	Outhaul _____
Luff cunningham _____	Leech cunningham _____
Main sheet _____	Boom angle _____
Sheet traveller _____	Leech line _____
Other items _____	
HEADSAIL _____	Halyard _____
Luff cunningham _____	Leech line _____
Sheet lead _____	Barber hauler _____
Spinnaker pole height _____	Pole angle _____
Permanent backstay _____	Runner _____
Kicking strap (vang) _____	Other items _____

Beaufort Scale: 6
Wind velocity: 21–26 knots (10.6–13 metres/second)
Pressure: 2.30 lb/sq foot (11.22 kilos/sq metre)

MAINSAIL

Small yachts have 1 or 2 reefs; others 1 reef. However large yachts will probably have no reefs, and others may have fewer reefs than stated, especially in sheltered waters and where other favourable factors apply.
Halyard: Tight, but not fully, to give ample sail camber.
Main outhaul: Tight out for maximum sail area.
Main sheet: Right out.
Main sheet traveller: Right off to leeward. Take in leeward tackle to absorb shock if yacht has to be gybed.

HEADSAIL

Medium spinnaker.
Halyard: Tight up.
Sheet: Lead to block well forward; trim spinnaker constantly to keep luff just not curling inwards. Spinnaker boom as far back as possible without sail collapse, and boom high. Clews level.

PERMANENT BACKSTAY

Slight tension, to reduce mast bend to minimum.

KICKING STRAP (VANG)

Tight down. Ease off if boom touches the water or boat starts to broach.

WINDWARD RUNNER

Just enough to cater for mast bend on masthead rig. Moderately tight on ¾ rig.

CREW POSITION

Well aft. Spread load athwartships to minimise rolling.

IT OFTEN PAYS TO TACK DOWNWIND, RATHER THAN RUN DEAD DOWNWIND.

BEST SETTINGS FOUND BY TRIAL:

MAINSAIL _____	Main reef _____
Main halyard _____	Outhaul _____
Luff cunningham _____	Leech cunningham _____
Main sheet _____	Boom angle _____
Sheet traveller _____	Leech line _____
Other items _____	
HEADSAIL _____	Halyard _____
Luff cunningham _____	Leech line _____
Sheet lead _____	Barber hauler _____
Spinnaker pole height _____	Pole angle _____
Permanent backstay _____	Runner _____
Kicking strap (vang) _____	Other items _____

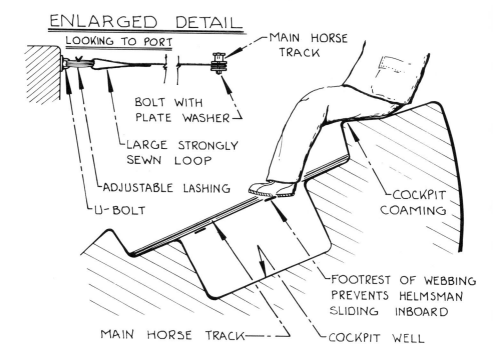

ENLARGED DETAIL
LOOKING TO PORT
MAIN HORSE TRACK
BOLT WITH PLATE WASHER
LARGE STRONGLY SEWN LOOP
ADJUSTABLE LASHING
U-BOLT
COCKPIT COAMING
FOOTREST OF WEBBING PREVENTS HELMSMAN SLIDING INBOARD
MAIN HORSE TRACK
COCKPIT WELL

HELMSMAN'S FOOTREST

No one can steer if they are not comfortable. When a boat heels even slightly, the helmsman wants to be sure he is not going to slither inboard. One way of making a light footrest is to use broad strong tape, like dinghy toe-straps. One end of the tape is fixed, possibly to the underside of the main sheet horse, and the other is adjustable by a lashing.

Beaufort Scale: 7
Wind velocity: 27–33 knots (13.5–16.6 metres/second)
Pressure: 3.60 lb/sq foot (17.58 kilos/sq metre)

MAINSAIL

Small yachts have 3 reefs, others 2 reefs, very large yachts may have 1 reef.
Top batten typically about 20° further off than boom.
Halyard: Tight up to about ⅓ breaking strain.
Main sheet: Tight down with boom off about 10°.
Main sheet traveller: Slide to leeward enough to angle boom 10° off yacht's
    centreline.

HEADSAIL

No. 3 genoa or working jib.
Halyard: Tight up to approx ⅓ breaking strain.
Sheet: Tight in till leech is near the shrouds, except in rough seas when it may
    pay to induce twist off at the top by leading the sheet further aft and possibly
    less tight in.
Barber hauler: Sheet lead angle off centreline of between 10° and 13°, further
    out in stronger winds.
Leech line: Just tight enough to avoid flutter.

PERMANENT BACKSTAY

Tension high, typically ⅓ of breaking strain for a straight forestay on masthead
    and ¾ rig.

KICKING STRAP (VANG)

Not needed, except sometimes, to flatten mainsail.

WINDWARD RUNNER

Moderately tight only, so that mast bends amply and flattens mainsail on
    masthead rig. Fully tight for a straight forestay on ¾ rig.

CREW POSITION

To windward and amidships.

BEST SETTINGS FOUND BY TRIAL:

MAINSAIL _____	Main reef _____
Main halyard _____	Outhaul _____
Luff cunningham _____	Leech cunningham _____
Main sheet _____	Boom angle _____
Sheet traveller _____	Leech line _____
Other items _____	
HEADSAIL _____	Halyard _____
Luff cunningham _____	Leech line _____
Sheet lead _____	Barber hauler _____
Spinnaker pole height _____	Pole angle _____
Permanent backstay _____	Runner _____
Kicking strap (vang) _____	Other items _____

Beaufort Scale: 7
Wind velocity: 27–33 knots (13.5–16.6 metres/second)
Pressure: 3.60 lb/sq foot (17.58 kilos/sq metre)

MAINSAIL

Small yachts have 3 reefs, others 2 reefs, very large yachts may have 1 reef.
Halyard: Tight up to about ⅓ breaking strain.
Main sheet: Tight down, but eased slightly in squalls or to reduce weather
    helm, and feather off top of sail.
Main sheet traveller: Boom off typically 20° but adjusted to suit course. Ease
    to leeward to reduce weather helm, especially in squalls.

HEADSAIL

No. 3 or No. 4 genoa or working jib.
Halyard: Tight up to approx ⅓ breaking strain.
Sheet: Ease off forward and outboard of close hauled position, with leech par-
    allel to mainsail.
Barber hauler: Ease outboard to avoid backwinding the mainsail.
Leech line: Amply tight, as flutter at this wind speed damages sail quickly.

PERMANENT BACKSTAY

Tension high, typically ⅓ of breaking strain.

KICKING STRAP (VANG)

Tight up.

WINDWARD RUNNER

Moderately tight on masthead rig to accord with mast bend. Fully tight on ¾
    rig.

CREW POSITION

To windward and amidships.

BEST SETTINGS FOUND BY TRIAL:

MAINSAIL _____	Main reef _____
Main halyard _____	Outhaul _____
Luff cunningham _____	Leech cunningham _____
Main sheet _____	Boom angle _____
Sheet traveller _____	Leech line _____
Other items _____	
HEADSAIL _____	Halyard _____
Luff cunningham _____	Leech line _____
Sheet lead _____	Barber hauler _____
Spinnaker pole height _____	Pole angle _____
Permanent backstay _____	Runner _____
Kicking strap (vang) _____	Other items _____

Beaufort Scale: 7
Wind velocity: 27–33 knots (13.5–16.6 metres/second)
Pressure: 3.60 lb/sq foot (17.58 kilos/sq metre)

MAINSAIL
Small yachts have 3 reefs, others 2 reefs. Very large yachts may have 1 reef.
Halyard: Tight up to approx ⅓ breaking strain.
Main sheet: Eased off till all tell-tales stream off, with boom out roughly 45°
    but to suit course. Ease off to reduce weather helm.
Main sheet traveller: Right off to leeward. Take in leeward tackle to absorb
    shock in case yacht has to be gybed.

HEADSAIL
No. 3 or No. 4 genoa or working jib, or heavy reacher.
Halyard: Tight up to approx ⅓ breaking strain.
Sheet: Ease off till headsail leech is parallel to mainsail, all tell-tales flying.
    Sheet lead will be forward and outboard of close reaching position.
Barber hauler: Right to leeward.
Leech line: Amply tight as flutter at this wind speed damages sail quickly.

PERMANENT BACKSTAY
Tension between ⅕ and ⅓ breaking strain, or to induce mast bend equal to
    about twice the mast fore and aft diameter.

KICKING STRAP (VANG)
Near tight up, but slackened off to ease leech of sail, to reduce weather helm
    and heeling. If much slackening is needed, this is probably a sign sail area
    needs reducing.

WINDWARD RUNNER
Moderately tight but eased just enough to cater for mast bend on masthead rig.
    Tight up on ¾ rig.

CREW POSITION
To windward and aft.

BEST SETTINGS FOUND BY TRIAL:

MAINSAIL _____	Main reef _____
Main halyard _____	Outhaul _____
Luff cunningham _____	Leech cunningham _____
Main sheet _____	Boom angle _____
Sheet traveller _____	Leech line _____
Other items _____	
HEADSAIL _____	Halyard _____
Luff cunningham _____	Leech line _____
Sheet lead _____	Barber hauler _____
Spinnaker pole height _____	Pole angle _____
Permanent backstay _____	Runner _____
Kicking strap (vang) _____	Other items _____

Beaufort Scale: 7
Wind velocity: 27–33 knots (13.5–16.6 metres/second)
Pressure: 3.60 lb/sq foot (17.58 kilos/sq metre)

MAINSAIL

Small yachts have 3 reefs, others 2 reefs. Very large yachts may have 1 reef.
Halyard: Tight up but not fully, to give ample sail camber.
Main sheet: Ease boom off to about 75° to centreline of yacht, then trim till all
   tell-tales stream.
Main sheet traveller: Right off to leeward. Take in leeward tackle to absorb
   shock in case yacht has to be gybed.
Boom foreguy: Should be fitted.

HEADSAIL

Heavy spinnaker, or No. 2 genoa. Small boats may set working jib, or No. 3
   genoa.
Halyard: Tight up.
Sheet: Trim spinnaker constantly if possible, but in practice it will probably be
   a case of setting sheet and guy so that the sail pulls constantly. Keep spinnaker clews level, spinnaker boom as far back as possible, with guy let to
   block well forward at deck edge. Genoa or working jib to be sheeted so that
   sail pulls constantly; this may involve sheeting sail to spinnaker boom end,
   with spinnaker boom on opposite side to main boom.
Leech line: Amply tight, as sail flutter in this wind speed damages sail quickly.

PERMANENT BACKSTAY

Tension to keep mast straight and not whipping.

KICKING STRAP (VANG)

Near tight up. Ease off to reduce weather helm.

WINDWARD RUNNER

Moderately tight to suit mast bend on masthead rig. Tight up on ¾ rig.

CREW POSITION

Aft and mainly to windward. Spread load to minimise rolling.

BEST SETTINGS FOUND BY TRIAL:

MAINSAIL _____	Main reef _____
Main halyard _____	Outhaul _____
Luff cunningham _____	Leech cunningham _____
Main sheet _____	Boom angle _____
Sheet traveller _____	Leech line _____
Other items _____	
HEADSAIL _____	Halyard _____
Luff cunningham _____	Leech line _____
Sheet lead _____	Barber hauler _____
Spinnaker pole height _____	Pole angle _____
Permanent backstay _____	Runner _____
Kicking strap (vang) _____	Other items _____

Beaufort Scale: 7
Wind velocity: 27–33 knots (13.5–16.6 metres/second)
Pressure: 3.60 lb/sq foot (17.58 kilos/sq metre)

MAINSAIL
Small yachts have 3 reefs, others 2 reefs. Very large yachts may have 1 reef.
Halyard: Tight up but not fully, to give ample sail camber.
Main sheet: Ease boom off to about 80° to centreline of yacht.
Main sheet traveller: Right off to leeward. Take in leeward tackle.
Boom foreguy: Should be fitted.

HEADSAIL
Heavy spinnaker or No. 2 genoa. Small boats may set working jib or No. 3 or No. 4 genoa.
Halyard: Tight up.
Sheet: Trim spinnaker constantly if possible, but in practice it will probably be a case of setting sheet and guy so that the sail pulls constantly. Keep spinnaker clews level and boom between 15° and 25° forward of square to the wind, with sheet overtightened to dampen rolling. Possibly set working jib inside spinnaker sheeted very flat to minimise rolling. Sheet and guy led to blocks well forward at deck edge. Genoa (or working jib set on its own) boomed out to windward on spinnaker boom.
Leech line: Amply tight, as sail flutter in this wind speed damages sail quickly.

PERMANENT BACKSTAY
Tension to keep mast straight and not whipping.

KICKING STRAP (VANG)
Tight down to prevent sail twist. Ease off to reduce weather helm, or if boom touches water or boat starts to broach.

WEATHER RUNNER
Moderately tight but eased just enough to cater for mast bend on masthead rig. Tight up on ¾ rig.

CREW POSITION
Well aft and spread out athwartships to minimise rolling.

IT OFTEN PAYS TO TACK DOWNWIND, RATHER THAN RUN DEAD DOWNWIND.

BEST SETTINGS FOUND BY TRIAL:

MAINSAIL _____	Main reef _____
Main halyard _____	Outhaul _____
Luff cunningham _____	Leech cunningham _____
Main sheet _____	Boom angle _____
Sheet traveller _____	Leech line _____
Other items _____	
HEADSAIL _____	Halyard _____
Luff cunningham _____	Leech line _____
Sheet lead _____	Barber hauler _____
Spinnaker pole height _____	Pole angle _____
Permanent backstay _____	Runner _____
Kicking strap (vang) _____	Other items _____

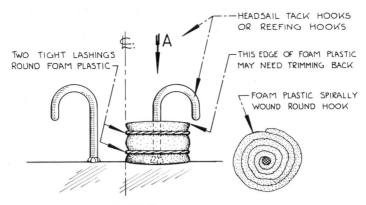

TWO TIGHT LASHINGS
ROUND FOAM PLASTIC

HEADSAIL TACK HOOKS
OR REEFING HOOKS

THIS EDGE OF FOAM PLASTIC
MAY NEED TRIMMING BACK

FOAM PLASTIC SPIRALLY
WOUND ROUND HOOK

KEEPING EYES ON 'PIGS' TAILS'

The bent metal hooks used for headsail tacks and to hold down the luff reef eyes of mainsails have one serious fault: they let the sail eye fall off before the halyard is tight up. To keep the sail safe, hooked onto the 'pig tail' hook, all that is needed is a piece of thin foam plastic. It is spirally wound round the upright part of the hook and acts like a spring closure, holding the sail on the hook until the luff is pulled tight.

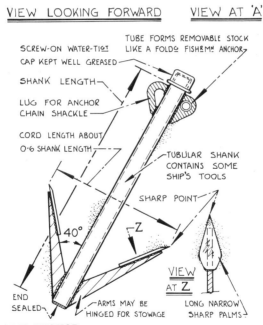

VIEW LOOKING FORWARD   VIEW AT 'A'

SCREW-ON WATER-TIGT
CAP KEPT WELL GREASED

TUBE FORMS REMOVABLE STOCK
LIKE A FOLDG FISHĘRMᴺ ANCHOR

SHANK LENGTH

LUG FOR ANCHOR
CHAIN SHACKLE

CORD LENGTH ABOUT
0·6 SHANK LENGTH

TUBULAR SHANK
CONTAINS SOME
SHIP'S TOOLS

SHARP POINT

40°

Z

VIEW
AT Z

END
SEALED

ARMS MAY BE
HINGED FOR STOWAGE

LONG NARROW
SHARP PALMS

WEIGHT SAVING ANCHOR

In some classes the weight of the anchor, or anchors, which have to be carried is specified. The anchor shown here is made too light, and its poundage made up by stowing some ship's tools inside the tubular shank.

This technique can be extended, so that the helmsman's seat cushion is a life-jacket, the boat-hook is the compulsory spare tiller, and the number 2 bilge pump can also be the toilet pump.

Beaufort Scale: 8
Wind velocity: 34–40 knots (17.2–20.1 metres/second)
Pressure: 5.4 lb/sq foot (26.36 kilos/sq metre)
Yachts with inexperienced crews often rightly give up racing at this wind speed.

MAINSAIL
Fully reefed, except on large yachts which may have 2 reefs.
Halyard: Tight up.
Main sheet: Trim till boom is off about 12°, or 1/4.5 of boom length. Top batten
   off about 20°.
Main sheet travellers: Ease off to suit above figures.

HEADSAIL
Working jib or, on small boats, storm jib. Large yachts set No. 4 or No. 5 genoa.
Halyard: Tight up to approx ⅓ breaking strain.
Sheet: Tight in till sail is near the shrouds, except in rough seas when it will
   probably pay to induce twist off at the top by leading sheet further aft and
   possibly less tight in.
Barber hauler: Sheet lead angle off centreline between 13° and 15°, further out
   in stronger winds.
Leech line: Amply tight to avoid flutter.

PERMANENT BACKSTAY
Tension high, typically ⅓ of breaking strain for a straight forestay and flat
   mainsail.

KICKING STRAP (VANG)
Not needed, except sometimes, to flatten mainsail.

WINDWARD RUNNER
Tight enough to stop mast whipping and to accord with mast bend on
   masthead rig. Tight up on ¾ rig.

CREW POSITION
To windward amidships.

BEST SETTINGS FOUND BY TRIAL:

MAINSAIL _____	Main reef _____
Main halyard _____	Outhaul _____
Luff cunningham _____	Leech cunningham _____
Main sheet _____	Boom angle _____
Sheet traveller _____	Leech line _____
Other items _____	
HEADSAIL _____	Halyard _____
Luff cunningham _____	Leech line _____
Sheet lead _____	Barber hauler _____
Spinnaker pole height _____	Pole angle _____
Permanent backstay _____	Runner _____
Kicking strap (vang) _____	Other items _____

Beaufort Scale: 8
Wind velocity: 34–40 knots (17.2–20.1 metres/second)
Pressure: 5.4 lb/sq foot (26.36 kilos/sq metre)
Yachts with inexperienced crews often rightly give up racing at this wind speed.

MAINSAIL
Fully reefed, except on large yachts which may have 2 reefs.
Halyard: Tight up to approx ⅓ breaking strain.
Main sheet: Boom off to approx 20°, but to suit course.
Main sheet traveller: Boom off typically 20° but adjusted to suit course. Ease
to leeward to reduce weather helm, especially in squalls.

HEADSAIL
Working jib, or on small boat storm jib. Large yachts set No. 4 or No. 5 genoa.
Halyard: Tight up to approx ⅓ breaking strain.
Sheet: Forward of close hauled position to keep tell-tales streaming when on
course.
Barber hauler: Outboard of close hauled position.
Leech line: Amply tight to avoid flutter.

PERMANENT BACKSTAY
Tension high, typically ⅓ breaking strain on masthead and ¾ rig.

KICKING STRAP (VANG)
Tight up, but ease in squalls to reduce weather helm.

WINDWARD RUNNER
Tight enough to prevent mast whipping and to accord with mast bend on
masthead rig. Tight up on ¾ rig.

CREW POSITION
To windward and amidships.

BEST SETTINGS FOUND BY TRIAL:

MAINSAIL _____	Main reef _____
Main halyard _____	Outhaul _____
Luff cunningham _____	Leech cunningham _____
Main sheet _____	Boom angle _____
Sheet traveller _____	Leech line _____
Other items _____	
HEADSAIL _____	Halyard _____
Luff cunningham _____	Leech line _____
Sheet lead _____	Barber hauler _____
Spinnaker pole height _____	Pole angle _____
Permanent backstay _____	Runner _____
Kicking strap (vang) _____	Other items _____

Beaufort Scale: 8
Wind velocity: 34–40 knots (17.2–20.1 metres/second)
Pressure: 5.4 lb/sq foot (26.36 kilos/sq metre)
Yachts with inexperienced crews often rightly give up racing at this wind speed.

MAINSAIL
Fully reefed except on large yachts which may have 2 reefs.
Halyard: Tight up to approx ⅓ breaking strain.
Sheet: Ease off till sail almost stalls. Accept lots of twist with top of sail fluttering intermittently. Move lead forward to limit excessive twist off.
Barber hauler: Right outboard.
Leech line: Amply tight to avoid flutter.

HEADSAIL
Working jib or storm jib. Larger yachts may set No. 4 or No. 5 genoa or heavy reacher.
Halyard: Tight up to approx ⅓ breaking strain.
Sheet: Ease off till sail almost stalls. Accept lots of twist with top of sail fluttering intermittently. Move lead forward to limit excessive twist off.
Barber hauler: Right outboard.
Leech line: Amply tight to avoid flutter.

PERMANENT BACKSTAY
Tight up, typically ⅓ breaking strain on masthead and ¾ rig.

KICKING STRAP (VANG)
Tight up, but ease to reduce weather helm or when the boom strikes the water.

WINDWARD RUNNER
Moderately tight to accord with mast bend and stop mast whipping on masthead rig. Tight up on ¾ rig.

CREW POSITION
To windward and aft.

BEST SETTINGS FOUND BY TRIAL:

MAINSAIL _____   Main reef _____
Main halyard _____   Outhaul _____
Luff cunningham _____   Leech cunningham _____
Main sheet _____   Boom angle _____
Sheet traveller _____   Leech line _____
Other items _____
HEADSAIL _____   Halyard _____
Luff cunningham _____   Leech line _____
Sheet lead _____   Barber hauler _____
Spinnaker pole height _____   Pole angle _____
Permanent backstay _____   Runner _____
Kicking strap (vang) _____   Other items _____

Beaufort Scale: 8
Wind velocity: 34–40 knots (17.2–20.1 metres/second)
Pressure: 5.4 lb/sq foot (26.36 kilos/sq metre)
Yachts with inexperienced crews often rightly give up racing at this wind speed.

MAINSAIL
Fully reefed, except for large yachts, which may have 2 or 3 reefs.
Halyard: Tight up to approx ¼ breaking strain.
Main sheet: Eased off till boom is about 75° to centreline, but to suit course.
Main sheet traveller: Right off to leeward. Take in leeward tackle to absorb shock in case boat has to be gybed.
Boom foreguy should be fitted.

HEADSAIL
Heavy spinnaker or No. 4 or No. 5 genoa or working jib. Storm jib on small yacht, possibly.
Halyard: Tight up.
Sheet: Spinnaker sheet led through a block well forward at deck edge, likewise guy. Spinnaker pole low and forward of 90° to the wind, by 10° or more. Genoa, working jib or storm jib sheeted to end of spinnaker boom tightly. Boom secured tightly with guy, topping lift and downhaul.
Leech line: Amply tight as sail flutter at this wind speed soon damages sail.

PERMANENT BACKSTAY
Tight up, typically ⅓ breaking strain on masthead and ¾ rig.

KICKING STRAP (VANG)
Tight up, but ease to reduce weather helm or when the boom strikes the water.

WINDWARD RUNNER
Moderately tight to accord with mast bend and stop mast whipping on masthead rig. Tight up on ¾ rig.

CREW POSITION
Aft and mainly to windward. Spread out athwartships to minimise rolling.

BEST SETTINGS FOUND BY TRIAL:

MAINSAIL _____	Main reef _____
Main halyard _____	Outhaul _____
Luff cunningham _____	Leech cunningham _____
Main sheet _____	Boom angle _____
Sheet traveller _____	Leech line _____
Other items _____	
HEADSAIL _____	Halyard _____
Luff cunningham _____	Leech line _____
Sheet lead _____	Barber hauler _____
Spinnaker pole height _____	Pole angle _____
Permanent backstay _____	Runner _____
Kicking strap (vang) _____	Other items _____

Beaufort Scale: 8
Wind velocity: 34–40 knots (17.2–20.1 metres/second)
Pressure: 5.4 lb/sq foot (26.36 kilos/sq metre)
Yachts with inexperienced crews often rightly give up racing at this wind speed.

MAINSAIL

Fully reefed, except for large yachts, which may have 2 or 3 reefs.
Halyard: Tight up to about ¼ breaking strain.
Main sheet: Off to about 80° angle to wind.
Main sheet traveller: Right off to leeward. Take in leeward tackle to absorb
shock in case boat has to be gybed.
Boom foreguy: Should be fitted.

HEADSAIL

Heavy spinnaker or No. 4 genoa, or working jib. Storm jib on small boat, pos-
sibly. If a spinnaker is set, a flat small headsail may be set sheeted tight
amidships to reduce rolling.
Halyard: Tight up.
Sheet: Spinnaker sheet and guy led through blocks at deck edge well forward.
Spinnaker boom low, and angled 20° forward of right angles to the wind.
Spinnaker sheet in overtight to minimise rolling. Genoa, working jib or
storm jib is sheeted to spinnaker boom end, the sheet being hauled in tight.
The boom is angled so that its outer end comes close to the sail clew. The
boom is secured by its uphaul, downhaul and the sail sheet, also possibly a
foreguy. On a large yacht the latter is essential.
Leech line: Amply tight as sail flutter at this wind speed soon damages sail.

PERMANENT BACKSTAY

Tight up, typically ⅛ breaking strain for masthead and ¾ rig.

KICKING STRAP (VANG)

Tight up but ease off to reduce weather helm or when the boom is striking the
water.

WINDWARD RUNNER

Moderately tight to accord with mast bend and stop mast whipping on
masthead rig. Tight up on ¾ rig.

CREW POSITION

Aft and spread out athwartships to minimise rolling.

BEST SETTINGS FOUND BY TRIAL:

MAINSAIL _____	Main reef _____
Main halyard _____	Outhaul _____
Luff cunningham _____	Leech cunningham _____
Main sheet _____	Boom angle _____
Sheet traveller _____	Leech line _____
Other items _____	
HEADSAIL _____	Halyard _____
Luff cunningham _____	Leech line _____
Sheet lead _____	Barber hauler _____
Spinnaker pole height _____	Pole angle _____
Permanent backstay _____	Runner _____
Kicking strap (vang) _____	Other items _____

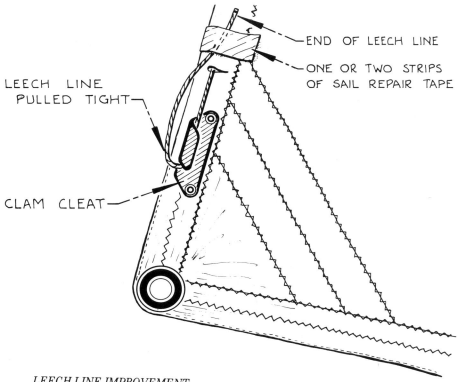

LEECH LINE PULLED TIGHT

CLAM CLEAT

END OF LEECH LINE

ONE OR TWO STRIPS OF SAIL REPAIR TAPE

LEECH LINE IMPROVEMENT

Leech lines get tangled up, especially in windy weather. Also they get whipped out of their clam cleats and so slacken off unless precautions are taken. A good way to secure the end of a leech line is to pull it upwards past the clam cleat and hold the line to the sail with a piece of sail repair tape. For heavy weather, it may be necessary to use two or three strips of repair tape.

Beaufort Scale: 9
Wind velocity: 41–47 knots (20.7–23.6 metres/second)
Pressure: 7.70 lb/sq foot (37.59 kilos/sq metre)
In open waters only experienced crews should continue to race to windward in this wind speed.

MAINSAIL
Fully reefed or trisail set.
Halyard: Tight up to about ¼ breaking strain.
Main sheet: Trim to have boom 12° off centreline, or 1/4.5 of boom length. Top batten off 20°.
Main sheet traveller: Ease off to suit above figures.

HEADSAIL
Working jib or on small yachts storm jib. Large yachts set No. 5 or 6 genoa.
Halyard: Tight up to approx ¼ breaking strain.
Sheet: Tight in till leech is near the shrouds, except in rough seas when it will probably pay to induce twist off at the top by leading the sheet further aft and possibly less tight in. In very rough sea conditions it will often pay to sail less close and hence have the sheet eased from the tight in position.
Barber hauler: Sheet lead angle off centreline between 13° and 15°, further out in stronger winds.
Leech line: Amply tight to avoid flutter.

PERMANENT BACKSTAY
Tension high, typically ¼ of breaking strain for a straight forestay and flat mainsail on masthead and ¾ rig.

KICKING STRAP (VANG)
Not needed.

WINDWARD RUNNER
Moderately tight to stop mast whipping and to accord with mast bend on masthead rig. Tight up on ¾ rig.

CREW POSITION
To windward and amidships.

BEST SETTINGS FOUND BY TRIAL:

MAINSAIL _____	Main reef _____
Main halyard _____	Outhaul _____
Luff cunningham _____	Leech cunningham _____
Main sheet _____	Boom angle _____
Sheet traveller _____	Leech line _____
Other items _____	
HEADSAIL _____	Halyard _____
Luff cunningham _____	Leech line _____
Sheet lead _____	Barber hauler _____
Spinnaker pole height _____	Pole angle _____
Permanent backstay _____	Runner _____
Kicking strap (vang) _____	Other items _____

Beaufort Scale: 9
Wind velocity: 41–47 knots (20.7–23.6 metres/second)
Pressure: 7.70 lb/sq foot (37.59 kilos/sq metre)
In open waters only experienced crews should continue to race to windward in this wind speed.

MAINSAIL
Fully reefed or trisail set.
Halyard: Tight up to about ¼ breaking strain.
Main sheet: Boom off to approx 20° but to suit course.
Main sheet traveller: Boom off typically 20° but adjust to suit course. Ease to leeward to reduce weather helm, especially in squalls.

HEADSAIL
Working jib or on small boat storm jib. Large yachts set No. 5 or 6 genoa.
Halyard: Tight up to approx ¼ breaking strain.
Sheet: Forward of close hauled position, and eased off just enough to keep sail full.
Barber hauler: Outboard of close hauled position, but only slightly as sail should be kept from 'lifting' along luff.
Leech line: Amply tight to avoid flutter.

PERMANENT BACKSTAY
Tension high, typically ¼ of breaking strain on masthead and ¾ rig.

KICKING STRAP (VANG)
Tight up, but ease in squalls to reduce weather helm.

WEATHER RUNNER
Moderately tight to accord with mast bend and stop mast whipping on masthead rig. Tight up on ¾ rig.

CREW POSITION
To windward and amidships.

BEST SETTINGS FOUND BY TRIAL:

MAINSAIL _____	Main reef _____
Main halyard _____	Outhaul _____
Luff cunningham _____	Leech cunningham _____
Main sheet _____	Boom angle _____
Sheet traveller _____	Leech line _____
Other items _____	
HEADSAIL _____	Halyard _____
Luff cunningham _____	Leech line _____
Sheet lead _____	Barber hauler _____
Spinnaker pole height _____	Pole angle _____
Permanent backstay _____	Runner _____
Kicking strap (vang) _____	Other items _____

Beaufort Scale: 9
Wind velocity: 41–47 knots (20.7–23.6 metres/second)
Pressure: 7.70 lb/sq foot (37.59 kilos/sq metre)
Yachts need careful handling to avoid damage at this wind speed.

MAINSAIL
Fully reefed or trisail set.
Halyard: Tight up to about ¼ breaking strain.
Main sheet: Eased off till boom is roughly 55° to centreline, but to suit course. Ease off to reduce weather helm, especially in squalls.
Main sheet traveller: Right off to leeward. Take in leeward tackle to absorb shock in case boat has to be gybed.

HEADSAIL
Working jib or storm jib. Larger yachts may set No. 5 or 6 genoa.
Halyard: Tight up to approx ¼ breaking strain.
Sheet: Ease off till sail almost stalls. Accept lots of twist off at the top, but limit twist off by moving lead forward from close reaching position.
Barber hauler: Right outboard.
Leech line: Amply tight to avoid sail flutter.

PERMANENT BACKSTAY
Tight up, typically ¼ breaking strain on masthead and ¾ rig.

KICKING STRAP (VANG)
Tight up, but ease off as necessary to reduce weather helm or when boom is striking the water.

WEATHER RUNNER
Moderately tight to accord with mast bend and to stop mast whipping on masthead rig. Tight up on ¾ rig.

CREW POSITION
To windward and aft.

BEST SETTINGS FOUND BY TRIAL:

MAINSAIL _____	Main reef _____
Main halyard _____	Outhaul _____
Luff cunningham _____	Leech cunningham _____
Main sheet _____	Boom angle _____
Sheet traveller _____	Leech line _____
Other items _____	
HEADSAIL _____	Halyard _____
Luff cunningham _____	Leech line _____
Sheet lead _____	Barber hauler _____
Spinnaker pole height _____	Pole angle _____
Permanent backstay _____	Runner _____
Kicking strap (vang) _____	Other items _____

Beaufort Scale: 9
Wind velocity: 41–47 knots (20.7–23.6 metres/second)
Pressure: 7.70 lb/sq foot (37.59 kilos/sq metre)
Yachts need careful handling to avoid damage at this wind speed.

MAINSAIL
Fully reefed or trisail set.
Halyard: Just tight up.
Main sheet: Eased off till boom is about 75° to centreline, but to suit course. Better sheeted in slightly too tight.
Main sheet traveller: Right off to leeward. Take in lee tackle to absorb shock in case boat has to be gybed.
Boom foreguy: Should be fitted.

HEADSAIL
Working jib or storm jib. Small boats should use a storm jib. A large well-handled boat sets a heavy spinnaker.
Halyard: Tight up.
Sheet: Spinnaker sheet led through a block well forward at deck edge, likewise guy. Spinnaker boom low and forward of 90° to the wind by 10° or more. Working jib or storm jib sheeted tightly to end of spinnaker boom, which is angled to suit sail clew position. Boom secured tightly with guy, topping lift and downhaul.

PERMANENT BACKSTAY
Tight up, typically ¼ breaking strain on masthead and ¾ rig.

KICKING STRAP (VANG)
Tight up, but ease to reduce weather helm or when boom is striking the water.

WEATHER RUNNER
Moderately tight to accord with mast bend and to stop mast whipping on masthead rig. Tight up on ¾ rig.

CREW POSITION
Aft and mainly to windward but spread out athwartships to minimise rolling.

BEST SETTINGS FOUND BY TRIAL:

MAINSAIL _____	Main reef _____
Main halyard _____	Outhaul _____
Luff cunningham _____	Leech cunningham _____
Main sheet _____	Boom angle _____
Sheet traveller _____	Leech line _____
Other items _____	
HEADSAIL _____	Halyard _____
Luff cunningham _____	Leech line _____
Sheet lead _____	Barber hauler _____
Spinnaker pole height _____	Pole angle _____
Permanent backstay _____	Runner _____
Kicking strap (vang) _____	Other items _____

Beaufort Scale: 9
Wind velocity: 41–47 knots (20.7–23.6 metres/second)
Pressure: 7.70 lb/sq foot (37.59 kilos/sq metre)
Yachts need careful handling to avoid damage at this wind speed.

MAINSAIL
Fully reefed or trisail set.
Halyard: Just tight up.
Main sheet: Off to about 75° to the wind.
Main sheet traveller: Right to leeward. Take in leeward tackle to absorb shock
   in case boat has to be gybed.
Boom foreguy: Should be fitted.

HEADSAIL
Working jib or storm jib. Small boats should use a storm jib. A large well-
   handled boat sets a heavy spinnaker.
Halyard: Tight up.
Sheet: Spinnaker sheet and guy led through blocks at deck edge well forward.
   Spinnaker boom low, and angled 20° forward of right angles to the wind.
   Sheet in overtight to minimise rolling. Working jib or storm jib sheeted
   tightly to spinnaker boom end. Boom angled to suit position of sail clew.
   Boom held by sheet, topping lift and downhaul.
Leech line: Amply tight as sail flutter at this wind speed soon damages sail.

PERMANENT BACKSTAY
Tight up, typically ¼ breaking strain on masthead and ¾ rig.

KICKING STRAP (VANG)
Tight up but ease to reduce weather helm or when boom is striking the water.

WINDWARD RUNNER
Moderately tight to accord with mast bend and to stop mast whipping on
   masthead rig. Tight up on ¾ rig.

CREW POSITION
Aft and spread out athwartships to minimise rolling.

BEST SETTINGS FOUND BY TRIAL:

MAINSAIL _____	Main reef _____
Main halyard _____	Outhaul _____
Luff cunningham _____	Leech cunningham _____
Main sheet _____	Boom angle _____
Sheet traveller _____	Leech line _____
Other items _____	
HEADSAIL _____	Halyard _____
Luff cunningham _____	Leech line _____
Sheet lead _____	Barber hauler _____
Spinnaker pole height _____	Pole angle _____
Permanent backstay _____	Runner _____
Kicking strap (vang) _____	Other items _____

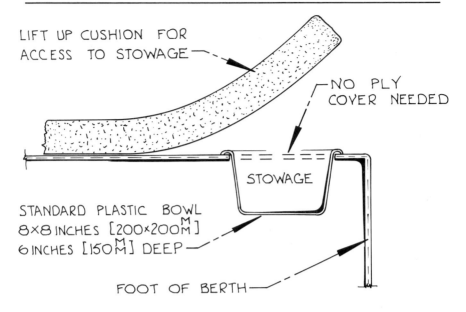

LIFT UP CUSHION FOR ACCESS TO STOWAGE

NO PLY COVER NEEDED

STOWAGE

STANDARD PLASTIC BOWL
8×8 INCHES [200×200M]
6 INCHES [150M] DEEP

FOOT OF BERTH

LIGHT WEIGHT STOWAGE LOCKER

Items like tools cannot be stowed in the bilge because they soon get wet, and they need to be handy. A quickly made locker consists of a plastic bowl, bought at any hardware shop, recessed into the top of a berth.

If the bowl is at the foot of the berth it does not need a cover because no one sits over it. The weight of a pair of feet does not seriously depress the berth mattress down into the bowl.

Beaufort Scale: 10 and upwards
Wind velocity: Over 48 knots (over 24 metres/second)
Pressure: Over 10 lb/sq foot (over 51 kilos/sq metre)
Only strong, well handled yachts should be raced at this wind speed.

MAINSAIL

Trisail. Large yachts may carry a fully reefed main. Small and medium sized
   yachts may beat with only a small headsail set.
Halyard: Tight up to about ¼ breaking strain.
Sheet: Trim to have boom 12° off centreline or 1/4.5 of boom length. Top bat-
   ten off 20°.
Main sheet traveller: Ease off to suit above figures.

HEADSAIL

Storm jib, or possibly no headsail, especially on small yachts. Large yachts
   may set working jib or very small genoa.
Halyard: Tight up to approx ¼ breaking strain.
Sheet: Tight in till leech is near the shrouds, on large yachts. Medium and
   small yachts will almost certainly have to have the sheet led well aft to spill
   wind from much of the top of the sail continuously, and the sheet should be
   eased till the sail is just working continuously.
Barber hauler: Sheet lead angle off centreline between 13° and 15°, and for
   small or medium sized yachts the latter figure or higher will be needed.
Leech line: Tight up to avoid flutter.

PERMANENT BACKSTAY

Tight up for a flat mainsail and straight forestay on masthead and ¾ rig.

KICKING STRAP (VANG)

Not needed, except sometimes tight up to flatten mainsail.

WINDWARD RUNNER

Moderately tight to stop mast whipping and to accord with mast bend on
   masthead rig. Tight up on ¾ rig.

CREW POSITION

To windward and amidships.

BEST SETTINGS FOUND BY TRIAL:

MAINSAIL _____	Main reef _____
Main halyard _____	Outhaul _____
Luff cunningham _____	Leech cunningham _____
Main sheet _____	Boom angle _____
Sheet traveller _____	Leech line _____
Other items _____	
HEADSAIL _____	Halyard _____
Luff cunningham _____	Leech line _____
Sheet lead _____	Barber hauler _____
Spinnaker pole height _____	Pole angle _____
Permanent backstay _____	Runner _____
Kicking strap (vang) _____	Other items _____

Beaufort Scale: 10 and upwards
Wind velocity: Over 48 knots (over 24 metres/second)
Pressure: Over 10 lb/sq foot (over 51 kilos/sq metre)
Only strong, well handled yachts should be raced at this wind speed.

MAINSAIL
Trisail. Large yachts may carry a fully reefed main. Small and medium yachts
  may set only a small headsail.
Halyard: Tight up to about ¼ breaking strain.
Main sheet: Boom off about 25° but to suit course.
Main sheet traveller: Boom off typically 25° but adjust to suit course. Ease to
  leeward to reduce weather helm, especially in squalls.

HEADSAIL
Storm jib, or possibly no headsail, especially on small yachts. Large yachts
  may set working jib.
Halyard: Tight up to approx ¼ breaking strain.
Sheet: Forward of close hauled position and eased off just enough to keep sail
  full.
Barber hauler: Outboard of close hauled position but only just, as sail should
  be kept from 'lifting' along luff.
Leech line: Amply tight to avoid flutter.

PERMANENT BACKSTAY
Tight up for a flat mainsail and tight forestay on masthead and ¾ rig.

KICKING STRAP (VANG)
Tight up, but ease in squalls to reduce weather helm.

WINDWARD RUNNER
Moderately tight to stop mast whipping and to accord with mastbend on
  masthead rig. Tight up on ¾ rig.

CREW POSITION
To windward and amidships.

BEST SETTINGS FOUND BY TRIAL:

MAINSAIL _____	Main reef _____
Main halyard _____	Outhaul _____
Luff cunningham _____	Leech cunningham _____
Main sheet _____	Boom angle _____
Sheet traveller _____	Leech line _____
Other items _____	
HEADSAIL _____	Halyard _____
Luff cunningham _____	Leech line _____
Sheet lead _____	Barber hauler _____
Spinnaker pole height _____	Pole angle _____
Permanent backstay _____	Runner _____
Kicking strap (vang) _____	Other items _____

Beaufort Scale: 10 and upwards
Wind velocity: Over 48 knots (over 24 metres/second)
Pressure: Over 10 lb/sq foot (over 51 kilos/sq metre)
Only strong, well handled yachts should be raced at this wind speed.

MAINSAIL

Trisail. Large yachts may carry a fully reefed mainsail. Small and medium
sized yachts may set only a small headsail.
Halyard: Tight up to about ¼ breaking strain.
Main sheet: Eased off till boom is roughly 55° to centreline, but to suit course.
Ease off to reduce weather helm, especially in squalls.
Main sheet traveller: Right off to leeward. Take in leeward tackle to absorb
shock in case boat has to be gybed.

HEADSAIL

Storm jib or possibly no headsail, especially on small yachts. Large yachts may
set working jib.
Halyard: Tight up to approx ¼ breaking strain.
Sheet: Ease off till sail almost stalls. Accept lots of twist off at the top, but limit
it by moving lead forward from close hauled position.
Barber hauler: Right outboard.
Leech line: Tight up to avoid sail flutter.

PERMANENT BACKSTAY

Tight up, typically ¼ breaking strain.

KICKING STRAP (VANG)

Tight up, but ease off as necessary to reduce weather helm or when boom is
striking water.

WEATHER RUNNER

Moderately tight on masthead rig to accord with mast bend and to stop mast
whipping. Tight up on ¾ rig.

CREW POSITION

To windward and aft.

BEST SETTINGS FOUND BY TRIAL:

MAINSAIL _____	Main reef _____
Main halyard _____	Outhaul _____
Luff cunningham _____	Leech cunningham _____
Main sheet _____	Boom angle _____
Sheet traveller _____	Leech line _____
Other items _____	
HEADSAIL _____	Halyard _____
Luff cunningham _____	Leech line _____
Sheet lead _____	Barber hauler _____
Spinnaker pole height _____	Pole angle _____
Permanent backstay _____	Runner _____
Kicking strap (vang) _____	Other items _____

Beaufort Scale: 10 and upwards
Wind velocity: Over 48 knots (over 24 metres/second)
Pressure: Over 10 lb/sq foot (over 51 kilos/sq metre)
Only strong, well handled yachts should be raced at this wind speed.

MAINSAIL

Trisail. Large yachts may carry a fully reefed mainsail. Small and medium
sized yachts may set only a small headsail.

Halyard: Tight up to about ¼ breaking strain.

Main sheet: Eased off till boom is about 75° to centreline, but to suit course.
Better sheeted in slightly too tight.

Main sheet traveller: Right off to leeward. Take in lee tackle to absorb shock in
case boat has to be gybed.

Boom foreguy should be fitted.

HEADSAIL

Storm jib or possibly no headsail, especially on small yachts. Large yachts may
set working jib or smallest genoa, but if very competently handled may set
smallest spinnaker.

Halyard: Tight up.

Sheet: Ideally sheet headsail to the end of the spinnaker boom, and haul sheet
in tight. The boom is angled so that its outer end is close to the sail clew. The
boom is secured tightly by its uphaul, downhaul and the sail sheet, also possibly a foreguy. On a large yacht the latter is essential.

Spinnaker sheet and guy: Led well forward at deck edge and boom well forward
of 90° to the wind.

Leech line: Tight up to avoid sail flutter.

PERMANENT BACKSTAY

Tight up.

KICKING STRAP (VANG)

Tight up, but ease off to reduce weather helm or when boom is striking water.

WINDWARD RUNNER

Moderately tight on masthead rig to accord with mast bend and stop mast
whipping. Tight up on ¾ rig.

CREW POSITION

Aft and mainly to windward but spread out athwartships to minimise rolling.

BEST SETTINGS FOUND BY TRIAL:

MAINSAIL _____	Main reef _____
Main halyard _____	Outhaul _____
Luff cunningham _____	Leech cunningham _____
Main sheet _____	Boom angle _____
Sheet traveller _____	Leech line _____
Other items _____	
HEADSAIL _____	Halyard _____
Luff cunningham _____	Leech line _____
Sheet lead _____	Barber hauler _____
Spinnaker pole height _____	Pole angle _____
Permanent backstay _____	Runner _____
Kicking strap (vang) _____	Other items _____

Beaufort Scale: 10 and upwards
Wind velocity: Over 48 knots (over 24 metres/second)
Pressure: Over 10 lb/sq foot (over 51 kilos/sq metre)
Only strong, well handled yachts should be raced at this wind speed.

MAINSAIL
Trisail. Large yachts may carry a fully reefed mainsail. Small and medium
  sized yachts may set only a small headsail.
Halyard: Tight up to about ¼ breaking strain.
Main sheet: Off to about 75° to the wind.
Main sheet traveller: Right to leeward. Take in leeward tackle to absorb shock
  in case boat has to be gybed.
Boom foreguy: Should be fitted.

HEADSAIL
Storm jib or possibly no headsail, especially on small yachts. Large yachts may
  set working jib or smallest genoa, but if very competently handled may set
  smallest spinnaker.
Halyard: Tight up.
Sheet: A headsail is sheeted to the end of the spinnaker boom. The boom is
  tightly secured with guy, topping lift and downhaul, the boom being angled
  to suit the position of the headsail clew. A spinnaker is kept as flat as possible with sheet and guy led to blocks well forward at the deck edge, boom
  well forward of 90° to the wind, and boom low.
Leech line: Tight to avoid sail flutter.

PERMANENT BACKSTAY
Tight up.

KICKING STRAP (VANG)
Tight up but ease off to reduce weather helm or when boom is striking water.

WINDWARD RUNNER
Moderately tight on masthead rig to accord with mast bend and stop mast
  whipping. Tight up on ¾ rig.

CREW POSITION
Aft and spread out athwartships to minimise rolling.

BEST SETTINGS FOUND BY TRIAL:

MAINSAIL _____	Main reef _____
Main halyard _____	Outhaul _____
Luff cunningham _____	Leech cunningham _____
Main sheet _____	Boom angle _____
Sheet traveller _____	Leech line _____
Other items _____	
HEADSAIL _____	Halyard _____
Luff cunningham _____	Leech line _____
Sheet lead _____	Barber hauler _____
Spinnaker pole height _____	Pole angle _____
Permanent backstay _____	Runner _____
Kicking strap (vang) _____	Other items _____

The sheet lead position for beating is normally near the aft end of the track. If there is more than one sheet lead track, it is normally the inboard one which is used for close hauled sailing, at least until the wind is above Force 6. The sheet is normally hauled in tight till the sail is close to the crosstree end. If there is more than one set of crosstrees, then the sail is tightened in till it is close to whichever crosstree it is going to touch first.

The aim is to get all the tell-tales, from top to bottom of the luff, flying together. If the lower tell-tales 'lift' off the sail when luffing, move the sheet lead aft along the track. Vice versa if the top tell-tales break away first.

There are 'rules of thumb' which can be used, for instance if the track leads very far aft (perhaps for a high clewed sail like a yankee). One such rule is:

The line of the sheet, when projected forward across the sail, should meet the luff half way between the head and the tack.

This rule needs modifying when the sail is mitre cut, or has one of the cuts with a lower seam which does not meet the leech at right angles. Then the line of the sheet, when projected forward, will be further down the luff. How much varies from sail to sail, but if in doubt, start with a point about 5% further down the luff. In practice this is likely to mean a shift aft of the sheet lead carriage (or car, or slide . . . there are too many names for this gadget!) by one or two holes in the track.

The exact location of the carriage will vary with wind speed, and with the amount of stretch in the sail.

Depending on the length and type of race, these preparations will be carried out a month, or at least two weeks before the race. However for a major race (such as a long distance offshore event) some of these jobs must be performed many months before the start.

Some jobs will have to be done twice. For instance if the boat is altered, the change may turn out to be a disaster, or it may have improved the boat but need further modifications.

1. Obtain race entry form.
2. Complete race entry form and post it, recorded delivery, with entry fee(s).
3. Book crew by phone or letter. Check they have passports and necessary visas for overseas races.
4. Send out crew instruction sheets (see page 61).
5. Make arrangements for boat to be taken to the starting area. Book marina space, or a place in the dinghy park, or a mooring for before the race.
6. Make plans for returning the boat to base after the race, including return delivery crew, or overland transport etc.
7. Buy charts and navigation books, also tide tables for the race area.
8. Check that the boat has an up-to-date measurement certificate or rating, or handicap, as appropriate.
9. Check that the boat conforms to the latest rules.
10. Ensure the boat is 'giving nothing away' due to excess weight or an unfavourable handicap which can be changed.
11. Arrange for the boat to be fully overhauled by:

    • Skipper and crew
    • Boatyard or independent boatbuilder
    • Mast specialist
    • Rigger
    • Engineer
    • Plumber
    • Electrician
    • Electronics expert
    • Winch specialist

12. Send sails for overhaul. Order new ones where needed.
13. Make sure all safety gear is on board. Confirm none of it will be out of date on the day the race ends, in case of delays. Send liferaft(s) for servicing. This needs to be done annually.

14. Make sure all technical literature is on board including:
    - Race event information
    - Racing rules
    - Navigation equipment manuals
    - Engine manual
    - Radio licence
    - Ship's papers etc.

    Have duplicates at home.
15. Where possible inspect rivals to see if they are stealing a march techni-cally.
16. Tune spars and rigging.
17. Try out all sails.
18. Have crew practice sessions. Make sure they are fit.
19. Swing compasses.

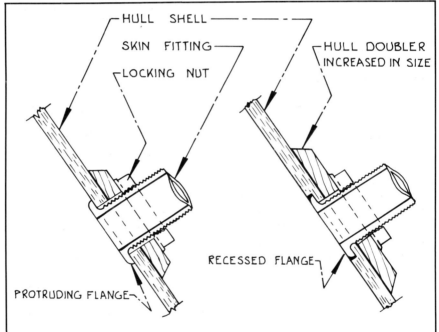

FLUSH SKIN FITTING

Protruding flanges on seacocks obstruct the smooth flow of water over a hull. Provided the hull is stiffened with a backing pad, or doubler, the flange can be recessed into a thick-skinned shell. Where the hull is not sufficiently thick, it is sometimes possible to partly recess the flange, and cautiously skim down the flange thickness.

These jobs will typically be carried out during the week before the race. However for a major race, some of this work must be done well before this. For a minor race, some of these jobs can be postponed until just before the event.

1. Phone round to check all crew members are fit and available.
2. Check that all work ordered at boatyard, sail loft, electronics specialist, rigger, winch specialist etc. has been completed. Pay their bills immediately, to ensure they are available at short notice in future.
3. Remove surplus weight and gear from boat.
4. Tape over, or re-tape: lifeline ends, shackle pins, rigging screws, crosstree ends etc.
5. Lubricate sheaves, snap shackles, spinnaker pole plungers, rudder bearings etc.
6. Start getting twice daily weather forecasts so that the approaching pattern and daily 'pattern repeats' can be detected.
7. Make a final check that the booked marina berth, or place in the dinghy park, or mooring, is available, for before and after the race.
8. Run engine to test it. Check its oil level, battery fluid level, gearbox oil level, stern gland grease cup level.
9. Prior to a long race clean out water tanks.
10. Check through all spares, safety gear etc.
11. Mark course on chart, with tidal information etc.
12. Check the starting watches and ship's clock. Run a daily check on the latter to find daily loss or gain.
13. Have boat scrubbed, and where necessary re-antifouled. Polish the bottom, check sacrificial plate(s), fair in dents, examine underside of keel and rudder, clear barnacles from log impeller(s) etc.
14. Back afloat, give mast and rigging final tuning check.
15. Check oil levels in hydraulic equipment.
16. Send someone aloft to check mast and rigging.
17. Finalise catering arrangements and put non-perishable food on board.
18. Clean boat externally and internally.
19. Pump bilge and clean it. Check all bilge pumps by opening them up. Clean strum boxes.
20. Test batteries in electronic instruments, check and calibrate instruments, do a radio check, etc.
21. Make sure all sail corners are marked with 'HEAD' 'TACK' or 'CLEW'.
22. Put spinnaker(s) in stops.
23. Ensure all sails are in correct bags, stowed in correct place.
24. Re-read race instructions to be sure nothing has been overlooked.
25. Lay in ample stocks for everyone on board of their favourite cigarettes, sweets and chewing gum.
26. Coax crew off alcohol in the final run up to the race.

Some of these jobs may be done 48 hours before the start, especially if the race is a particularly long one. Because gear can be temperamental, especially electronic equipment, some items on this list also appear on the list of jobs to be done a week before the start.

1. Take seasickness tablets well before the start.
2. Get a weather forecast, or more than one. A forecast 12 hours, 6 hours and just before the start should show a definite pattern.
3. Check that all crew are on board, with their gear.
4. Make sure crew know where all gear is stowed.
5. Move sails to racing location on board.
6. Put waterproof covers on cushions.
7. Put out first chart(s) to be used. Check other charts are in the order in which they will be used.
8. Load exactly the correct amounts of food, water, and fuel.
9. Ensure everyone gets the correct type of meal at the right time, through the day.
10. Run engine, check battery etc.
11. Screw down stern gland greaser when engine is finally stopped.
12. Make arrangements to be towed to start line by a 'chummy ship' in case engine fails on run to the start. Agree to do the same for 'chummy ship'.
13. Pump bilge and mop it dry.
14. On a large yacht send a man aloft for final check.
15. Look over chart of the course in the light of the latest weather predictions.
16. Close all seacocks except those which will be needed, such as the engine cooling water intake.
17. Check navigation instruments, batteries, lights, life-buoy lights etc.
18. Pull down spare halyards, replacing them with light messenger lines, to reduce weight aloft.
19. Ensure all halyards are on the correct side, with no twists aloft (notably on the headsail halyards) and that all snap shackles are working well.
20. Move aft end of topping lift forward, or replace it with a messenger line (but not if it is needed for reefing).
21. Deflate inflatable dinghy and stow it ashore or below.
22. Remove sail cover(s), boat hook and loose deck gear. Stow these ashore or below.
23. Reeve off sheets, guys, spinnaker boom downhaul etc.
24. Check round waterline for fouling.
25. Put winch handles in correct pockets.
26. Put lifebuoys in the on-deck position if they are kept below when on moorings.

27. Recheck time of high tide, also flow directions and speeds for whole race.
28. Start up navigation instruments, put in waypoints, calibrate as necessary etc.
29. Hoist class flag.
30. Depart for the start in ample time to allow for contingencies such as: an unusually strong tide; halyard accidentally let go aloft; dirt in the engine fuel etc.
31. Shut all hatches and opening ports, remove vent cowls etc.

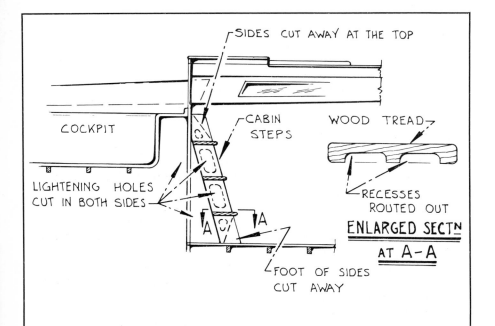

CUTTING OUT SURPLUS WEIGHT

By slicing off surplus wood, or metal or plastic, weight can be saved, often without even a small loss of strength. This sketch shows how the sides of the cabin steps can be trimmed off at top and bottom, and large lightening holes cut between the treads. The flat steps may be drilled full of holes, or routed out on the underside, as shown in the enlarged section on the right.

These techniques can be applied to all sorts of components, from cabin sole boards to fiddles, from berth bases to door-posts.

Some starts involve more preparation than others, depending on the size of boat, space on the water, length of race and so on. As with the other lists, the following needs to be adapted to the circumstances.

1. Arrive at the starting line in ample time.
2. A friendly wave to the starting officers acknowledges they are giving their time for your enjoyment.
3. Start reading the wind speed and direction from the moment the boat arrives at the starting area. Look for regular shifts, or a steadily veering (or backing) wind, or a steady increase or decrease.
4. Get a weather forecast on the radio.
5. Ensure the crew are properly dressed, in oilskins or as appropriate.
6. Check all instruments are working properly.
7. Run a test on the stopwatch. Rewind it after the test.
8. Get the course from the committee boat or shore station.
9. Mark the course on the chart.
10. Punch in the waypoints and run the course computer etc.
11. Set the correct sails for the course, and have the probable changes near to hand.
12. Have the probable spinnaker made ready, also its gear.
13. Check all sheets and guys are running free and have end knots to prevent them running out of their blocks (except spinnaker sheet).
14. Check tidal current by observing its flow past buoys, the moored committee boat etc.
15. Ensure centreboard and drop rudder are in the correct position, normally fully down for the start.
16. Sail up the first leg with crew in correct positions. Note speed, compass heading on both tacks, boat trim etc.
17. Observe wave patterns on left and right sides of course.
18. Check current at windward mark if it can be reached with ample time to get back to the start.
19. Make a series of trial starts, noting compass course on both tacks.
20. Note what other yachts are doing, and note their choice of starting location.
21. Align propeller shaft so that propeller blades are in position of minimum resistance, normally with blades vertical.
22. Apply propeller shaft brake.
23. Watch performance of boats in classes starting earlier.
24. With all the available evidence the tactician, navigator and helmsman should discuss the best starting procedure, possibly also consulting the crew.

25. Start time checks with the stopwatches as early as possible, using previous class starts as checks.
26. Make sure all members of the crew have their favourite cigarettes, sweets and chewing gum to hand.
27. In light airs stay close to the line.
28. Cross the starting line at the best possible speed.

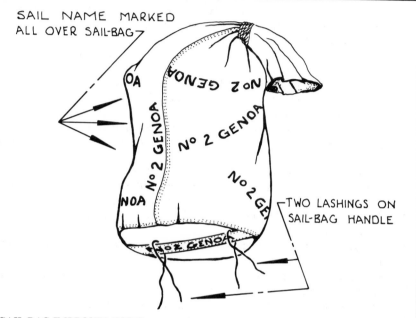

SAIL NAME MARKED ALL OVER SAIL-BAG

No 2 GENOA

TWO LASHINGS ON SAIL-BAG HANDLE

SAIL BAG IMPROVEMENTS

Sailmakers usually mark the name of a sail only once on its bag. The name is all too often on the side of the bag hidden from view. This does not help someone in a rush to find a particular sail in a dimly-lit cabin.

Using an indelible marker, it is easy to put the name on the bag all over and all ways up, so that it is easily read regardless of how the bag is lying.

The two lashings on the base help when securing the bag down so that the sail can be pulled out easily.

1. Discuss the race, making sure everyone on board contributes.
2. Enter up the Race Log with date, course, weather, other boats, route over the course, sails set, precise settings to halyard tensions, outhaul tension etc, lessons learned, improvements for the next time the conditions are similar, etc.
3. List breakages and worn items for repair or replacement before the next race.
4. List food, water, fuel, oil, toilet paper, paper roll for the galley, chart pencils, instrument batteries etc needed for the next race.
5. Take down class flag.
6. Replace vent cowls which have been taken off.
7. Check hydraulics, clean and dry cylinders and rods. On moorings take off all loads. Check oil levels.
8. Ship topping lift, boom gallows etc.
9. Put on sail covers.
10. Unreeve and stow below: sheets, guys, spinnaker boom downhaul etc.
11. Stow below items which will weather, or which may be stolen: lifebuoys, winch handles, liferaft, etc.
12. Pack up perishable food.
13. Turn off: engine fuel cock, all seacocks, main battery switch(es), all instruments (after doing a battery check).
14. Pump the bilge.
15. Clean boat inside and out.
16. Padlock deck lockers and take precautions against thieves.
17. Shut all hatches, opening ports etc.
18. Take sails to repairers.
19. Thank the race officers (whatever you thought about the course set); without their freely given time there would be no racing.

CREW JOINING INSTRUCTIONS

(The 'form' opposite will need altering to suit different boats. It is usually photocopied so that the owner has enough copies for all the crew for a whole season's racing. That is, for a normal crew of 6 taking part in 10 races run off 60 copies plus spares, say 80 copies. It was originally developed by John Illingworth, though it pre-dates the inclusion in his book *Offshore*.